To Bryn
I HAVE A Glimps
of How Biblical
Deborah!
Thank U

Un-Coloring Race

BLACK TO B'REISHEET

Testimony of a Black Christian American

JEFF S. MORTON

2023

Un-Coloring Race

BLACK TO B'REISHEET

Testimony of a Black Christian American

JEFF S. MORTON

PRINTED IN THE UNITED STATES OF AMERICA
First Printing

Unless otherwise indicated, Scripture quotations are from the American King James Version, Produced by Michael Peter (Stone) Engelbrite, November 8, 1999.

And

The New King James Version. Scripture taken from the New King James Version. Copyright © 1982 by Thomas Nelson, Inc. Used by permission. All rights reserved.

Cover Design: Art Palecek, used by permission
Design & Layout: Lanitta Jaye Delk
Illustrations & Charts: Lanitta Jaye Delk
Logo Design: Jimmie Christiansen
Editor: Marlene Y. Bastian

ISBN 1453841156
EAN-13 9781453841150

Un-Coloring Race
BLACK TO B'REISHEET

Testimony of a Black American Christian

JEFF MORTON

Acknowledgements

This is my first attempt at writing an entire book. Always up for a challenge, this would be a piece of cake, or so I thought! The number of people who literally joined me in this effort as well as the contributions they made, and the corrections that caused me to learn a few things, happened continuously.

For example, Pastor Mark Biltz (my pastor) of El Shaddai Ministries has added to thirty-five years of my faith a weekly explosion of "Ah Ha" moments. It is astounding what comes out of his understanding of the scriptures. Art Palecek also is my pastor and friend. He offered to design the cover of this book. The finished product took my breath away. Art captured what I was thinking perfectly. Dora the "Torah Explorer," thank you for your computer paper, your ink cartridge, and your time!

To the congregation of El Shaddai Ministries, you all are simply the best! To Al, Tommie, and Jeff Cooper of GLC, I want to be present when the King of kings crowns you all for the work you are doing. You, along with all of the folks at God's Learning Channel (Prime Time Christian Broadcasting), change lives.

To Valerie Jolie, I know now what a rock solid friendship with the opposite sex is all about. I simply adore your faith and your food! Thanks to my friends Gloria Jackson and Cheryl Lewis of Los Angeles, California. You both have spent long hours, asked many questions, and offered much revelation on both the phone and the computer. Gloria, dinner is on me when I come to California.

To the teachers of Torah and the Gospels, may the spirits of Elijah and of Moses continue to show to you the unlimited God of Glory so that you can continue to show it to us. To my editor, Marlene Bastian, thank you, thank you, thank you! To Vince and Jan Jahrman, thank you for the encouragement and suggestion to write this book. To Lanitta Jaye Delk, you made this book happen, thank you so very, very much!

To my sisters: Desi, it is not possible for you to know how much I appreciate the entire gift that you represent to my life and Gina, may you continue blessing people everywhere, everyday. To my brothers: Rodney, Jamie, Brian and David, we have been scattered too long! This was never the Father's plan.

To Dan and Brenda Cathcart, you both represent to me how Yeshua brings his people back together (thirty+ years later in our instance). Thank you for your support throughout this effort. To Kenny and Tony, thanks for the groceries and keeping me overweight. To my mother, thank you for your prayers and for being our gladiator, forever fighting for the lives of your kids. YOU'RE THE BEST!

To Ryan Anderson:[1] Thank you for keeping the website up and running. I bet you'd like to get paid regularly! Stay in my life man! To Carroll Gleason of Carroll Gleason Productions, thank you, my friend, for your support and expertise. So many people are supporting me and this effort. I am finally...very, very humbled!

Special acknowledgment

To Mr. & Mrs. Kirk Keppler and Mr. & Mrs. David Strelinger. From the depth of my spirit, thank you for allowing me to find sanctuary in your families.

To my Pastor, my Friend and my Mentor, Mark Biltz: Nearly four years ago YHVH used you to "Blow my mind." You can stop at any time now! (smile) I have grown to look forward to the Sabbath at El Shaddai Ministries almost as much as HIS return. Shalom, Shalom, my brother, to your whole house. G'mar Chatima Tova

---

1. http://www.ryancanderson.com

Dedication

I dedicate this book to my kids.

Anthony Allen, you're our strength.

Julia Renee, you're our laughter.

Kyle Zachary, you're our reflection.

Myklen Capree, you're our inner power.

Remember the consequences!

I hope that I have pleased you,

Adonai Ye-Ho-VaH

Table of Contents

Genesis 26:5

Because that Abraham obeyed my voice, and kept my charge, my commandments, my statutes, and my laws.

Introduction

In this book, I share some of the difficult experiences in my life, as well as the wonderful experiences of becoming a person of faith, but it contains so much more. I realize that we all are like a puzzle that must be connected according to the way our creator specified. What we have done over many, many years is to become disconnected. As you read, I am confident that you will find we share similar experiences. Our differences allow us to become connected.

In a manner of speaking, every puzzle offers this challenge. Like a puzzle, when every piece is connected the image is revealed, restored, intact. We are the image of our Savior. This book is asking us to obey all the commandments, and most importantly... to love one another. To realize that this is the final goal has not changed. You will find previous articles I have written peppered throughout the chapters in this book. I think the next book, should there be another, will catalog those articles.

I almost cannot breathe at times because I want to share so much of what has been happening in my life, particularly in the last few years. The changes I have experienced during the last four years alone are beyond anything I could have thought or dreamed. At times painful memories interject themselves into my thoughts, but they do not have the control, nor do they arrest all that is happening today. Pain often is one of our worst enemies and the hardest thing to let go. I am not allowing myself to focus on those areas of my past nor am I allowing those events to keep me from sharing with you this most amazing time in my life! I do not live in my scars, and neither should you.

So many world wide phenomena are occurring now that it is hard to keep up. This has left many people I have come into contact with plodding along through life feeling defeated and/or depressed, or both, but not me! I am full of expectation, and a kind of joy that elevates in magnitude lives through me every second of every day of my life!

Although I am writing this book for many reasons, *you* are the number one reason. I am hoping to release some of this joy into you, and hopefully into the lives of others as well. I simply am thrilled to have the opportunity to do this. I also am very humbled.

The coming King of our world is wrapping presents for all of us. His delight in those who hear his voice is what motivates him. We are that motivation in one way or another. I pray that you experience a surprise while reading this book. The surprise concerns his identity. His identity is imprinted into the history of a particular people. Their culture, language, and very existence all are at the center of everything that is created and happening in the world today. All is in full restoration mode. The light switch that illuminates what we all have missed has been turned on.

My identity was born out of the thoughts of the one who created all this experience. The first part of this book is about how I grew up and what happened to me along the way. To be very clear, I believe in a creator, a divine being. His name is Yeshua (Jesus Christ), as I prefer to call him by the name given by the angel of the Lord to his earthly mother, Mary or Miryam. Yeshua means "Salvation" in Hebrew.

My identity also is defined in Him and I celebrate this experience, this journey. I do not look at it as a muddled series of failures and disappointments (although there are many of those), but rather as an awakening as to why I am here in the first place. My salvation is intact as I celebrate him in these pages.

This book, among other things, is about coming face to face with deception. Not the sort of deception that Christianity taught me about the devil (Satan), although I will be addressing the *prosecutor* as well. (He has an arsenal of tools designed to rob from us, kill us, and destroy us.) However, I also am referring to the tools we use against one another.

We define ourselves quite differently than what was intended. We use race and religion to justify our bigotry and prejudices. We use social status to subjugate some, while we berate others. We have taught ourselves to use a variety of tools against one another as well. I know about these tools, and have used many of them against others. My personal story (testimony) is willingly shared with you, in part, in the beginning of this book. I did not always have a changed heart.

Before we go any farther, please know that what is most exhilarating to me at 51 years of age is the joy overflowing from the root of my

4

story. Yeshua (Jesus Christ) is that root! He also is the root of all Judeo-Christian faith. Through him, I am forgiven, and I claim every promise he made to mankind. I now understand the joy that caused him to bear the stripes on his back for our healing, and his willingness for his blood to be shed at the *Mount of Olives* to pay the penalty for our sin once and for all. But this is not all he did.

I have peered into the "Jewishness" (if you will) of our coming King, and realize this part about my Lord was not taught to me. Yes, the Lion of the tribe of Judah is Hebrew, and now I understand His delight in me. Furthermore, I understand the depth of what "FAMILY" is all about. I understand why too many are broken, including my own.

I share the testimonies found in these pages, although they no longer define me. Who I am becoming still is evolving. Life flows through my experiences; I no longer am bound by them. I no longer am trapped, defeated or depressed. You are about to find out why.

For the past three and a half years, I leap out of my bed each day looking to tell someone, anyone, about the Lion of the tribe of Judah. This is not done from a witness or evangelical concept but rather from joy in my heart. It is my time to share what one shares when the fullness of our creator is realized in a person's life.

I know how King David felt when he danced before Yeshua. I feel the pounding in my chest and the excitement tearing at my soul. I understand more about His word, His promise, and His purpose. The Messiah has been illuminated beyond what I had known these past thirty-five years.

Our King is unlimited and so, too, is His word. If you don't yet know Him, then you are being robbed! If you only know Him from Christianity, then you very likely are being short-changed, and don't know it. See what happens when and if you should challenge what you have always known, or simply never known. This book will help you to do so.

I was no different. I was robbed. I have been stolen from and destroyed. (I use these terms figuratively for the purpose of illustration.) The prosecuting angel does not change nor deviate from his playbook. Lucifer, the angel of deceit, is doing what he was created to do, prosecuting mankind for not hearing and obeying our Savior, who continues to walk with all of us, both the saved and unsaved. Our King is committed to our salvation.

The devil, Lucifer, Satan, or however you wish to refer to him, is like a page number in a book. (How many of you purchase a book so as to read the page numbers?) Like the pages in a book, this created angel is found on almost every page of our lives. His purpose is to make sure we know about the commandments of Elohim that we are not keeping. He is not our Savior's nemesis or competitor. To think that Lucifer is *"all that and a bag of chips"* is simply delusional. The ability given to this angel is experienced only in our breaking covenant and not keeping the rules. (Who among us has never broken a covenant?)

For the record, I have realized the world is an amazing place, not because of what we are doing in it, on it, or to it, but because of why we were born to be here in the first place. Hopefully, what I have to share will help you understand that as well.

Some may ridicule or slander the message of this book, not understanding its intended message. Hopefully, others will find meaning, and possibly even relate to my story. However you receive this work, I wrote it for you. I am living what I am sharing in this book. I am experiencing the *something new*, the *something amazing*.

Life is concrete, tangible, and purposed, an opportunity miraculously tailored for each individual. It is a personal revelation waiting for self-discovery. Life is full, so very full, of redemption.

The absoluteness of why we are here is startling. I see all of life like an IMAX movie playing across the heavens. The Bible, each word, continually exposes the illnesses of living separated from the source.

My life is at a point where the fallen world can't take from me anymore. Sinful living cannot undo all that is being done in and with my life as I look deeper into the root of the plan. You see, I no longer am sick. The plan of redemption is medicine to those needing a cure. It is more than hope that stares back at me. I see an invitation with my name written on it.

To quote the words written by singer and songwriter Steven Curtis Chapman: *"We've been invited with the Son, and we've been invited to come and believe the unbelievable, receive the inconceivable, and see beyond our wildest imaginations. Lord, we come with great expectation."*

Even though deception continues to try and rob from us all, it cannot crush the spirit. Disobedience does that. In this book, I am trying my best to explain to all of you how to see deception for what it is. However, I have one request before you continue: **Un-Color yourself.**

Skin color is not what separates us from one another, it is sin! Our invitation to life comes to us by way of Israel. If you do not know who these people are, it is most likely because you were taught to not know them at all. It may well be that deception is just as alive in how we came to know the Gospels as well. This book will challenge 1,800 years of history and well it should. The restoration of the House of Jacob (Israel) and the reclamation of Yeshua's bride were set into motion at the cross.

We are the most beautiful, most imaginative wonder in all of creation. Although Israel is the Jewel the creator of heaven and earth chose as his own special people, he left the door open to us all. Cast off the lie that says otherwise, for we all are descendents of dirt, made in the image of Yeshua. Everything in this world made by man came from dirt.

We are witnessing "The Greatest Story Ever Told!" Step out from the divisions of race and religion. Grasp the reality (if you choose to participate) that you are a *Kid of the Kingdom,* colorless, unbroken, a child of purpose, draped in untold beauty. Step out from the veil of deception long enough to realize you and I also are chosen people who can choose to accept the redemption offered through Yeshua which brings us to forgiveness of sin and restored fellowship with our Creator.

Walk through these pages of my story, peeling off the colors of your own story when you see the need to do so. You may not experience anything more than reading another book. I hope that this is not the case because I guarantee that your life needs to be freed from the divisions that keep us all from loving in the way we are loved by God himself.

Let me share with you how I was able to do it. It started with the following questions, "Lord, why were you Jewish?" and "Who is Judah?"

This book is not about exposing what is wrong with all of us. The concept of hearing and then doing is as old as mankind. Like the covenants, you have to recognize your obligations. Prejudice against any one of the world's inhabitants is breaking covenant and certainly disobeying a commandment.

If you despise Jews, Black folk, Muslims, Christians, or anyone else, you have been blinded to the truth. You are not a free person. You are being robbed, but also you are cursing almost everyone in your path.

If you are willing to journey beyond that sort of thinking, this book will show you there is hope and help to change – if you will believe it. If you continue reading this book, I pray you will be blessed and enlightened, and will un-learn the lies we all inherited and believed.

The Messiah is coming out of the box we put him in. He is asking all of us to choose once again.

Jeremiah 16:19 (AKJV)

O LORD, my strength, and my fortress, and my refuge in the day of affliction, the Gentiles shall come to you from the ends of the earth, and shall say, Surely our fathers have inherited lies, vanity, and things wherein there is no profit.

I pray you see this little, tiny, blue earth that we all inhabit as a miracle and not just a dirty, messy little planet that we keep screwing up.

Why we are here is the miracle!

8

The Gospel through Names Listed in Genesis

The numbers displayed after the # symbol are Strong's Exhaustive Concordance reference numbers.

Adam: *Mankind*
#120: 'adam' (aw-dawm) from 119; ruddy i.e. a human being (an individual or the species, mankind, etc.)

Seth: *Is appointed to*
#8352. Sheth, (shayth) from 7896; put, i.e. substituted; #7896. Shiyth, (sheeth) a primitive root; to place (in a very wide application):–apply, appoint, array, bring, consider, lie (up), let alone

Enos: *Feeble, frail, mortality*
#582. 'enowsh, en-oshe' a mortal (and thus differing from the more dignified 120); hence, a man in general (singly or collectively); #605. 'anash, aw-nash' a primitive root; to be frail, feeble

Cainan: *A fixed Dwelling place*
#7018. Qeynan, kay-nawn' from the same as 7064; fixed. #7064. qen, kane contracted from #7077; a nest (as fixed), sometimes including the nestlings; figuratively, a chamber or dwelling:–nest, room

Mahalaleel: *God who is praised*
#4111. Mahalal'el, mah-hal-al-ale' from 4110 and 410; praise of God

Jared: Comes down, descends
#3382. Yered, yeh'-red from 3381; a descent; #3381. dry yarad, yaw-rad' a primitive root; to descend

Enoch: *To instruct, train up*
#2585. Chanowk, khan-oke' from 2596; initiated. #2596. chanak, khaw-nak' a primitive root; properly, to narrow (compare 2614); figuratively, to initiate or discipline: –dedicate, train up

Methusalah: *A man sent forth*
#4968. Methuwshelach (meth-oo-sheh'-lakh) from 4962, 7973; man of a dart. #4962 math, math from the same as 4970; properly, an adult (as of full length); by implication, a man. #37973. Shelach, from 7971; a missile of

attack #7971. shalach, (shaw-lakh') a primitive root; to send away, for, or out

Lamech: *To be beaten, smitten, and tortured*
#3929 from #4347. makkah, mak-kaw' or (masculine) makkeh (muk-keh');
(plural only) from 5221; a blow; by implication, a wound; figuratively,
carnage, also pestilence: –beaten, blow, plague, slaughter, smote, X sore,
stripe, stroke, wound((-ed))

Noah: *Bringing rest, a quiet peace*
#5146 Noach, (no'-akh) the same as 5118; rest. #5118 nuwach, (noo'-akh)
or nowach (no'-akh); from 5117; quiet

The meanings of the names read as follows:

Mankind / is appointed to / feeble, frail, mortality / a fixed dwelling place
/ God who is praised / comes down / to instruct / as a man sent forth / to
be beaten smitten and tortured / bringing rest, a quiet peace.

Preface

Exodus 15:26

And said, If you will diligently listen to the voice of the Lord your God and will do that which is right in His sight, and will give ear to His commandments, and keep all His statutes, I will put none of these diseases on you which I have brought on the Egyptians, for I am the Lord that heals you.

Beyond Encouragement

It is said of me by two friends and also my pastor, "Jeff, you are like the town crier." I have many, many friends who have seen such a dramatic change in me, and how I now understand many scriptures. (Sadly, I have lost several friends as well.) I attribute this change to something that occurred nearly four years ago.

A quick summary:

One day in church, I was listening to yet another pastor toss the Jews under the bus. The sermon was addressing the book of Galatians, where Paul was talking to a group of people who were of the Hellenistic persuasion. For the most part, the people from Galatia did not know about Judaism or the TORAH, but did know well about Zeus and the gods of Greek mythology. I was curious about this, so while sitting there in church, I quietly inquired of the Lord "Why are the Jews blamed for just about everything?" A quiet whisper of a voice replied "I was one of them; learn about my Jewishness."

11

Prior to this experience, I had studied about Israel, but my studies always were of a political nature. I knew about prime ministers and generals during the rebirth of the nation. I knew about the ancient kings and the many, many periods of Jewish history concerning rebellion and disobedience. Certainly, I knew about biblical accounts of the Jews, but I avoided Judaism at all cost because I was a Christian and would not go there! What I did not know much about were the Hebrews and the families that were born through them.

Later, I attended a conference called "Convergence Northwest." A man at that conference asked me "Have you ever seen the gospel in Genesis?" For the sake of brevity, I direct you to one particular page on my website: http://www.hearandobey.us/?page_id=1116

In the moment I recited what this man had written down, the Lord, in a supernatural manner, poured into my brain the understanding of why he came as a Jew. The man, whom I did not know at the time, was Pastor Mark Biltz of El Shaddai Ministries. (It is virtually impossible for me to explain this occurrence to you. I also have tried on numerous occasions to relate that millisecond in time to others, without much success.)

Yahweh poured into my whole being the signs of what he is doing, found only when one sees why he poured his identity into the Jews. He is Torah. Many others who have shared about who he is have missed the mark, and Christianity turned Him into a Greek god. (I say this with diplomacy.) Over 30,000 doctrines are found in Christianity about our Savior. Since receiving this insight from the Lord, I have been bouncing off the walls of my life.

In the meantime, I have lost virtually everything I had, including my home, my career, and most of my family. I have struggled to be employed, and as is the case with many, many Americans, I have been through some of the most difficult times of my adult life. In the midst of all this, however, I have *joy*!

Many of us see life as difficult, painful, and coming with a variety of highs and lows.

Certainly mine is no different, except for one gigantic occurrence, which keeps me in a constant state of joy. I am joyful beyond description, which is to many who have an intimate knowledge of my life, an oxymoron.

One day, nearly four years ago, the Lord showed me who He was in His word and in the signs represented in his celestial universe. The signs are repeated in His biblical Festivals, and most amazing of all, the history of the Jewish people. They are the descendants of Judah. Our Messiah is the Lion of the tribe of Judah.

I look at the Bible that the so-called "blind" Jews wrote, and realize He is alive through these people, through His word, and through the pages that reveal Him daily from century to century. You simply must know His *Hebrew nature* or He becomes only an endless search through scripture, as opposed to a constant revelation of unlimited majesty.

He has shown me that this is not the end times, but rather the birth of eternity, Zion, and His reign with His people in the Father's house. He has shown me the coming coronation and elevation of the suffering priest to the King of Kings and Lord of Lords. He shows me daily the Lion of the tribe of Judah, and that this birth is happening.

I see the chaos among men as the reason His Father's house must be cleaned, renewed, and restored. I see the wedding preparations commencing, while the world is resisting. I see the glory of the King of the Jews as He prepares for the great day of the Lord! I can hardly breathe at times because every day I see His word shredding the foundations of those who refuse to hear and obey His commandments. I see Satan roaring like a lion, a counterfeit, while the Lion of the House of Judah is preparing to roar like nothing in all of creation. How can anyone not be filled with expectation?

The creator of Adam has called out to me by name, and showed me signs and wonders. They start with the air I breathe, the light I see, and the glory of every day I am afforded. I see the wonders of His hand in every second of my existence. This life is amazing! I could have been made a rock hanging out in the Grand Canyon or worse, under a porch, but even the rocks will cry out his name. Such encouragement! I wish I could stop bouncing off the walls for a few minutes.

Horrible, utterly devastating events are soon to take place in this world. The only difference between those which have occurred before us and now is that we are the ones who must endure! Our generation is the one Moses was speaking of in Deuteronomy 32. Daniel was looking at us, and so too was Zechariah! They tell the story because the Lord is coming. They share the visions of the resistance that screams against His throne. I suppose I am a town crier, a watchman on the wall (like so many today). However, I do not believe in doom and gloom, but rather the glory of the coming of the King!

Where is your heart and where is your allegiance? The question all we who believe need to ask is, "How do I act in His presence?" He soon will be here. "Prepare ye the way of the Lord" in your life. Be encouraged as you prepare to meet your King, your husband, the son of the Father, the Living Word, Yeshua the Messiah.

In June 2009, after I had flown to Texas to do an interview, the Lord awakened me from sleep to tell me He wants people of color to *Un-Color* themselves. This now is what I spend every waking moment sharing with all who will listen. The Lord did not color us to be ugly and bitter. Like the colors of the rainbow and the beauty of why we are dazzled by it, this is what he had in mind for us as well. Those who believe are believing it because they are saved, grafted into the covenants with . . . Israel. *He was Jewish* for many, many, many reasons.

If you are saved but hate Israel, something is out of balance in your faith. If you keep Torah but disregard Yeshua, you, too, have a problem. The curses following this sort of thinking are evident in the entire world. Be encouraged, the covenants are still in play and keeping the commandments still needs to be done (We have yet to do our part).

Un-color your religion.

Jeff Morton
http://www.hearandobey.us
Amen

14

Chapter One:
Coloring My Childhood

Exodus 16:28

And the Lord said to Moses, how long refuse you to keep my commandments and my laws?

I know virtually nothing about the relationship between my mother and father, but I certainly am able to recall some horrific stuff. Most children carry such episodes through life as if they are waving a flag or banner.

My parents married in Spring Lake, New York in 1956. The marriage produced four sons and one daughter. My father came from a family of fourteen, including his parents. Mother was a twin. Her family had fourteen children. For the most part, both families were close among themselves. Growing up, I knew most of my cousins and other relatives. We were a large family at the time, and have become considerably larger. Many are unknown to me these days, as I mostly have lived outside of New York for the past 34 years.

I was born in 1959 in the little village of Lyons, New York, which is located in Wayne County, upstate from New York City and nearer to Auburn. Most of the small villages in this area have been around since the early 1800's. I don't know much about any of their histories or communities. Based upon all my childhood memories, New York State seemed to be the place I had to escape from. I never have truly embraced the fact that New York is home, particularly Rochester.

Auburn was a fun place. We would go there to visit relatives every once in a while. My mother spent most of her years in Auburn, while my father hailed from Savannah, New York. Mom said my father's family was from Spring Hill, New York. Prior to writing this book, I did not know Spring Hill existed.

One of my mother's older sisters married into the McLeod family of Auburn, New York. The McLeod family grew up a few doors away from Harriet Tubman's home, which was a small white house with a rickety picket fence. I actually was able to go through the home as a child. I don't remember much, although I do recall quite clearly a picture of Harriet Tubman, a photograph of her sitting in a lone chair. She was aged, the photo was black and white, and very old but framed. I remember the inscription on the frame, which read "Black Moses."

My fascination with historical things was born as a result of this visit. I was in awe, and I remember feeling special that day. It was as though I somehow was connected to this woman and the history of her life. I have always remembered visiting her home.

The home is restored today, owned by the A.M.E. church, according to information on the world wide web. It does not look like the house I saw as a child. However, I did find one online image of the house I remembered. Seeing that picture resulted in the connection to Harriet Tubman from my childhood happening all over again.

Most of my memories of life in New York are not filled with many moments like these wonderful ones; they are very few indeed. Our father was not part of our visits to Auburn.

In 1965, I was six years old, and from the top of the stairs I could hear my mother telling my father if he came through *that door* she would blow his head off. At that time, we were living at 94 Prospect Street in Rochester, New York. I was the third oldest child and even at that tender age I knew our mother meant what she said to our father. My two older brothers and I were huddled together at the top of the stairs; our mother was facing down our father, and pointing a loaded revolver at the front door. We could not see him from our position, but we could see mom. We could sense her resolve; she was tired of being beaten, thrown down the staircase, or dragged through the house kicking and screaming, always fighting our father.

This night my brothers and I knew that mom was never going to be picked up like a sack of potatoes and thrown into a dry bathtub again. (I actually had witnessed this event.) Somehow I knew my dad was about to be gone forever. We had seen so much violence, so much pain. Our mother seemed always to be fighting our father, trying to defend herself against his abuse. Thinking about it all these years later, I realized our mom always fought back. My siblings and I were spectators, the audience. Mom was the "gladiator" throughout my childhood. A childhood filled with pain.

On this particular night, Mom had the upper hand. Her voice was different; she was calm and rational. I believe our mother was collected and self-assured in this moment, while our father was a breath away from "making her day!" I still am able to feel the anxiety and adrenaline of this moment. We all have moments in time that stay with us for a lifetime. This was certainly one of them, permanently etched into our young minds. The same feelings and clarity of emotion race through my whole being even now, as I relive the image of that big, shiny, dark blue handgun pointed at my daddy! Our father left that night, and I did not see him again until I was seventeen years old. We never called him *daddy* again.

I remember moving to 94 Prospect Street, although I am not sure how long we were living there before the gun incident. That house was a sanctuary at the time.

Prior to moving there, our family had been separated. My mother, younger brother, younger sister, and I had been living with my uncle and his wife in a duplex at 7 Draper Street, also in Rochester, New York while my two older brothers were living with our father's mother. (The two youngest had yet to be born.) Today, we are seven siblings all of whom still are alive.

The duplex was grey in color and the only house on our side of the street. It was sandwiched between the Department of Public Works truck and maintenance facility and a furniture store. The furniture store had apartments above it. In one of those apartments lived a little girl, my first love. Her name was Mariah, and her mother became our babysitter. I was just five years old, and I had a crush on this "little angel." Mariah was my only friend in those days. As she was a little bit younger than me, she could not yet go to school. This presented a few problems for our relationship.

The Department of Public Works (DPW—the acronym I don't recall figuring out until reaching my thirties) was brown in color. It was a dark, foreboding, and ominous place with an asphalt landscape. Broken beer and soda bottles were so numerous that the asphalt itself had a shimmer in the sunlight. There were no trees or flowers, and weeds grew out from the bases of the telephone poles. The smell of trash and creosote, along with diesel fumes, filled the air around this gigantic garage where crusty blue collar workers regularly would yell, "Get the hell out of here, kid!"

A little old black man with yellow eyes would walk from door to door, pulling a chain as though he was climbing a ladder. As he was pulling, up went the steel doors and out came the trucks, which I counted every day before school. "One, two, four, five, nine, ten, eleven, three, seven..." I had no idea they were garbage trucks, only that they were funny-looking trucks that had a foul odor. This was my "Sesame Street" (before Sesame Street was created), and where I first learned to count.

All of the grown-up folks referred to this place as the DPW and it became my playground. On weekends, I could play in the parking lot; it was right next door. No trucks, no people, no-one to yell "Get out of there!" I don't remember any of the games I invented, or things that poured through my imagination. I only remember I did not want to be in "that house." I was always wanting to get out of it.

This lonely duplex tucked into this part of our ghetto represents to this very day one of the worst experiences of my childhood. In the other unit lived a family who became my "living hell" for the remainder of the time we lived there. Their children were much older than me. The daughter was sixteen or so. She had two older brothers, one of whom abused me for as long as we lived at 7 Draper Street.

We lived through the race riots of 1964. I thought the adults were going to burn down our neighborhood. Policemen followed mobs of black people down our street, beating them with sticks and using dogs to bite and hurt many in the crowds.

Most of the horror that took place during these riots was a few streets away on Joseph Avenue. I did not know what Joseph Avenue was at the time, but I did know people were always fighting up on that street. It seemed to me that the street was lined with liquor stores and burned out buildings. There were more people congregating on the corners than living within the homes that stood like images from a war, although most of the homes were occupied.

I became afraid of the police during that time. They were the enemy. The Paddy Wagons (as we called them back in that day) would drive up and soon the rear doors would open and vicious dogs (to me anyway) would come out. It was horrible! In the eyes of a little boy experiencing abuse, everyone in the streets were fighting. (This is how life appeared to me at the time.) Some people were black, others were white; all were separated by skin color. The dogs seemed to know on instinct who to bite. They did not bite the white people. White folks at that time and age of my life were police or people who did not like us. This is how I knew that the city was different. (Thank God that my school teachers were different.) We watched all this from the upstairs window. (We had to sneak into that room because my uncle and his wife slept in there.)

It was during these riots that the older kid from next door seemed to be in our house often (while the adults were out rioting or trying to go to work). He was perhaps 17 or 18 years old. The police never came and took him away. Nobody stopped him from hurting me.

I hated that duplex. Everything about living there was evil! A good portion of my childhood died while living at 7 Draper Street.

Switching back to Prospect street, have you ever lived in a house that had a basement wall collapsed adjacent to the city sewer? Well, this was just such a place. I remember waking up one night to our mother pounding an empty 16 ounce Pepsi soda bottle against the floor. She was positioned between my brother and me. The bottle was the type that sort of "twisted" as it neared the spout and was very thick glass, as I recall. (They stopped making those bottles years ago.)

It took a few moments for my eyes to adjust to what actually was happening. Momma had a sewer rat by the tail! She was killing it with the bottle. I had seen that look in her eyes many, many times before. Mother had a way of expressing "How Dare You" in the way she tackled disobedience. That poor rat was supposed to stay in the basement. Our warrior, our *gladiator*, was at it again!

Our basement door was a trap door on the first floor near our only bathroom. The bathroom walls were painted "hot pink" and the room was dimly lit. It was the most frightening room in the entire house, and the trap door just outside the bathroom led to a place of horror. No one ever went down there. The basement was always dark and always full of water. Can you imagine walking through this house and down the stairs to the bathroom in the middle of the night as a six year old?

Our family was at war with the rats. We all shared the same battlefield. I don't think I ever saw the hole in the wall where the sewer rats had access. I knew it was there, although I never went down there. Whenever the trap door was lifted, I would try to peer down into the dark abyss that was our basement. Mom would yell, "Get out of there!" I always was adventurous and curious, and I wanted to see the war zone.

I really have no idea how long we lived in that place. I do remember that Dr. Martin Luther King, Jr. was murdered, and how distraught all the adults became. After reading much concerning Dr. King, I feel sure he would have approved this book.

My mother's youngest sister purchased her first car, a 1969 olive green colored Pontiac Firebird. She loved that car so much she later purchased a 1973 bright red Pontiac Firebird Trans Am with a firebird emblem painted on the hood, which I later stole. I happened to be at her house that day, hanging out with my cousin. I was 14 at the time and on vacation from George Junior Republic.

My aunt's red Trans Am was wooing me and taunting me. I asked her if I could wash it one day when she was visiting another sister. She never treated me the same after I stole her car.

That same aunt died a few years ago. (You learn how to deal with loss as you go through life; however, this loss was truly difficult.) The youngest of 14 children was lost to us all in a split second. This aunt had introduced me to regret. I wish I could take back the time that I stole her car. I could never do that, and she let me know it for the rest of our relationship.

I remember the day my mother called to tell me of her death. I was shopping at one of those stand-alone bread stores, a place where one could get more for less money. (I often shopped there because I had many mouths to feed besides mine--my wife, our four children, two dogs and two cats, my *family*.) I was there, stocking up. I always kept plenty of food in my home, possibly a reaction from reflecting back to the way things were in my childhood.

I recall collapsing up against a shelf, cell phone pressed against my ear as I heard my mother tell me that her kid sister was dead. I remember gasping, "Oh, no!" I truly needed support in this moment. Momma knew this would be tough for me to hear. My favorite relative was gone! I was not even able to attend her funeral. (Writing this book has forced me to re-live some very painful memories. The tears cascading down my face proved this to be so as I walked back through my life.)

Living on the West Coast for many years has had its disadvantages. Even as I was writing this chapter of the book, a family reunion on my father's side of the family was to take place in Rochester, New York. I would have loved to be there, but it simply was not doable.

Time seemed to stand still in the days of my youth. Rioting often took place during the summers, and snow storms (blizzards, really) were part of the winters. My childhood was similar to those of most kids living in our ghetto; survival was what we all were striving for. Each day provided another lesson for us. In actuality, those years flew by.

Odd how we move through the pages of our lives, suppressing thoughts and memories that have helped mold us. I continue to learn that life is a series of twists and turns, and discovery! The things that we suppress have the strongest hold on how we think, how we do everything. These are the very things that color our pain.

I finally told my mother about what happened to me at 7 Draper Street when I was twelve years old. Mom held me in her arms and said, "I am so sorry."

I also became sexual with girls at a very early age. I don't recommend this behavior to anyone. All I want to say about this is that our creator has a perfect plan about how to enjoy the beauty of loving someone in a very intimate and purposeful way.

I was robbed, like many other kids nowadays. We reach for the apple, and reap the hell that comes with it. We don't even think there are consequences to many of the things we do today. It is much more difficult for kids to embrace morality these days, as so many are being abused in one way or another.

The colors that define people also are so separated that we truly are abstract. I can recall the artists who tossed a bunch of paint onto a canvas, as if they were tossing mud. When they were finished and out of breath, they had the audacity to stand back and call it *art*.

We do similar things to one another, calling it multiculturalism. I consider this to be a modern form of segregation and separation, and I call it terrible! How many of you know your neighbors, and how many of you care about them?

What we don't realize is that at some point in our experiences, almost all of us have to "un-train" pain. The first part of my life was being introduced to it! Knowing how to love one another and to know our neighbors becomes frightening, as opposed to appreciated. We become separated from the second of the ten commandments rather quickly.

FIRE

You may already know this, but the Western mind (culture) is very linear. We have learned to analyze through deductive reasoning, as well as trial and error. This all is based on our evolution from Greek to Roman societies. Without going into greater detail, much of what happened as a result offers a sort of belief system about how things are defined. The various philosophies and sciences, or both, have become the basis of much of the discussions about how things work.

Hebrew culture is based upon patterns and repetition. This is how our creator reveals himself to us all. Hebraic thinking is finding a sort of revival in how to look at what there is to look at, and to see what can be seen. The patterns are on display in just about everything. In order to understand what this section is attempting to show you, one has to go back to the beginning.

In Hebraic thought, everything is circular, repeated, or evidenced through patterns. The concepts found in the very days of the week repeat, as do the months of the year. Summer returns to summer, winter to winter, etc.

Our sun is another example, and possibly the best one to use. The sun has several planets that circle it. This has been going on since before any of us understood what the sun is. It is a gigantic ball of fire centered in our galaxy. The relationship the earth has with the sun is very unique. No other life, so far, has been found on the other planets. Our planet has an abundance of life; brilliant forms of living creatures cover this globe.

We have discovered fire on this planet. The sciences tell us that fire must have oxygen, fuel, and a heat source, or ignition. Without air, fire cannot exist. Without fuel, it cannot burn. Without heat, it is not fire. Moses saw fire.

Exodus 19:18

"And Mount Sinai was altogether on a smoke, because the LORD descended upon it in fire: and the smoke thereof ascended as the smoke of a furnace, and the whole mount quaked greatly."

In fact, fire is mentioned many, many times in the bible. Much of our understanding of the presence of the Lord involves fire. Often, the biblical patriarchs could not look upon it, touch it, or stand in its presence. If I were to go outside and look up at our sun, it would be for mere seconds. The eyes simply cannot look upon it without great damage occurring. The body cannot stay exposed to it for very long without experiencing significant damage. If the sun were a bit closer or further from the earth, life on our planet would not exist.

The bible tells us that God is with us, always.

Matthew 28:20

"Teaching them to observe all things whatever I have commanded you; and, see, I am with you always, even to the end of the world." Amen.

Well, the sun came before philosophy and science. It needs no air to exist, no fuel and no heat, as evidenced by the very fact there is no air, no fuel, and no heat supplying its energy in the center of our galaxy. If the sun ever stops burning, we all stop living. I think it is easier to simply admit that all of life circles this fantastic ball of fire in the center of our galaxy as opposed to ignoring the inexplicable miracle because of scientific analysis. Perhaps it truly is time to go back to the basics, or the beginning.

The Son came to us through the Hebrew people. He is returning to the same. Perhaps it is not fire, which keeps us all alive after all. Obviously, a nuclear explosion needs no air, but mankind did not create either. We simply discovered how to do it.

Chapter Two:

GJR
(George Junior Republic)

Exodus 20:6
And showing mercy to thousands of them that love me, and keep my commandments.

Everyone was "black and proud" in my neighborhood. We were trapped in the early 70's at the time. Many were wearing dashikis, cheap medallions around our necks, and most teenage boys reeked of *Brut* cologne. We would put the medallion over our afros as if we were trying to thread a needle. Heaven forbid we mess up the perfect afro! Bell bottom jeans and hot pants were as common in the black neighborhoods as were the Number 10 cans of meat and government cheese lining most pantries.

Our shoes were colorful; they were called *platforms*. They were the stupidest things on the earth. Mine were black and red! I would slide into those shoes with the four-inch heels and the four-inch soles, and at the same time slide into *cool*. It was like going from Clark Kent to Superman.

I had a new identity. That identity caused me to meet a man in a long black robe. Here come the judge!

I was standing before a judge in Monroe Country Juvenile court. (I was not wearing *those shoes* at the time.) There I was, looking up at this judge who, in my mind, was seated up really close to the ceiling. He looked to be ten feet tall, or at least the desk or perch he was sitting on seemed to be. The room was all white. Fluorescent lighting made the whole scene look cosmic to me. I might as well have been standing there in a straight jacket. I felt trapped, exposed, caught!

I had just turned thirteen years old. One could only steal so many cars, I suppose. My probation officer, Don Simkin, was sitting behind me with my mother. There I was, facing a new character, and Perry Mason was not defending me. The Judge was to me a real live television character, and a cartoon, in my rebellious mind. His robe somehow gave me the feeling that he was important. Nevertheless, the fact that he was a man who appeared to have authority was unconvincing to me. After all, what was male authority to me?

Another twist in my adventure occurred on this day; my curiosity always was penetrating the situation. The judge ordered me to be locked up, *off to see the wizard*, only instead of *Oz* he lived at the Monroe County Juvenile Detention Facility of Rochester, New York.

I spent 30 days in this place. A friend of mine was in the detention center also. His name is Rodney. We all called him Boo-Boo. He shot a teacher (who recovered) several weeks earlier at our high school, Madison High School, if memory serves me correctly. Boo Boo was famous! In those days, shooting a teacher was unheard of. Bringing a gun to school was unheard of. The idea that this kid was on every news channel, and was the talk of the whole city, was actually weird now that he and I were locked up. I was not like him; of course not! He and I bonded together, something about prison life, I guess. The thing I remembered the most about Boo Boo is that he was a kid just like me. Both of us always knew this about each other; we simply had nothing to prove.

One day Boo Boo walked into the bathroom. One of the other kids was murmuring in the toilet stall, door closed. He was a scrawny little white boy. I don't remember his name. This young boy was in the process of being molested by another kid, an older boy. Boo-Boo came and found me. Together we stopped what was happening and made it known to the staff. On this day, a wounded, highly emotional boy (me) was able to do something about a memory that had haunted me for several years. For the first time in my life, I had victory over those memories; we were heroes.

Imagine for a moment two young boys, one who had shot his teacher, and the other who was emotionally stunted by an event of abuse earlier in life, as heroes for the first time ever. Doing the right thing always comes with benefit.

I fell in love while in the detention center. A pretty little Puerto Rican girl and I sat together during meals. (The girls were housed on one side of the facility, the guys on the other. Mealtime was the only time we could spend with the girls. She was so cute. Her name was Millie. (Momma would have said she was *fast*.) Millie was light-skinned. She had a curly afro some days. Other times her hair was pulled tight into a big pony tail. Millie was gorgeous!

It seems to me so many years later that she was in there for running away. Millie was a child prostitute. She had a pimp and the whole nine yards! One day, Millie wasn't at lunch – she was gone; I never saw her again. A few days later, Boo-Boo was gone. I never saw him again either.

I never saw the wizard again either, but thirty days had come and gone and it was back to the fluorescent lights and the larger than life cartoon. The same Judge asked, "Well, young man?" He did not seem so tall, and his voice was kinder. I wanted to thank him.

Don Simkin drove me to George Junior Republic located in Freeville, New York. GJR (as I still affectionately call this place) is beautiful. Tucked into the hills near Ithaca, New York and not too far from Cayuga Lake was this wonderful place that God himself had set aside for me. The campus was spread out across the landscape, with dazzling fall colors rolling out before me. It was October; everywhere the eye could see was beautiful. Several houses dotted the hillside. None of the homes sat next to one another as they did back home. This place was fabulous! A post card had come to life. This is where my real adventure began.

27

While driving to this wonderful place, Mr. Simkin explained to me my IQ was such that placing me into a juvenile facility for delinquent kids would be unproductive. He was the nicest man I had known up to that time. Don Simkin was one of the first people during my youth who had both talked to me and listened. (I would have given anything in this world if I had been able to say *Thank You* to this man.)

Mr. Simkin and I paraded through the various offices of GJR. Several people referred to me as a *Ward of the Court*. Whatever that meant didn't much matter to me; curiosity was sitting in the base of my throat. Suffice it to say GJR was a game changer. I spent several years there. They were not all easy. The thing I learned the most while at GJR was that I was not alone. The world was full of screwed up kids. I realized that white kids whose families had money had the kind of problems that only money could buy. Many of the white kids were products of much of the same sort of problems we all grow up with. They were raped, physically abused, or simply thrown away. Many of the kids were tucked away because money could afford to do just that. Only a few of them, if memory serves me correctly, were introduced to GJR through the court system.

For the most part, the black kids were from the inner cities of New York, New Jersey and Pennsylvania. We all had one common trait; none of us were brain dead. Based on various stories I can remember, the abuse many had experienced was incredible. My story is relatively minor compared to some of the horrible life experiences they shared. We all were just a bunch of kids trying to survive! It's strange how we end up doing some of the same things as adults.

GJR was co-ed at the time. For the first time in my life, I began to feel like a person. I began to experience me, as a result of coming in contact with those other kids. This was a time of great discovery for me. I never experienced racism at GJR, although I consider one particular teacher to be a jerk; I remember him well. Regardless of this individual, George Junior Republic became a sanctuary ordered by my heavenly Father, of this I am certain. If it had not been co-ed, I probably would have avoided a few problems (since I did like the girls).

The school was set up like a community or village. For example, we had a banking system complete with a bank, a courthouse, and a jail.

28

There were other such community entities as well. The bank had tellers, the court had a judge, and the jail had a warden. A member of the student body filled each of the positions, including all the judiciary positions. This was true in almost every instance in our miniature republic.

We went to school half days; the rest of the time we were involved in trade schools. The adults supervised everything. We had real teachers, and a real school system recognized by New York State. For the most part, the kids learned how to coexist within the community by literally working together. The various special positions were earned by performance and merit. I don't recall if we had a voting system or elections. (Odd how that memory escapes me.)

I do recall stacking hay. I simply hated this part of GJR. Working on the farm was miserable. I was a city boy! The memory even now is best compared to eating something foul, or rotten; yuck! One hot summer day a bunch of us kids were stacking the hay into one of the barns. We had to tier it up in a manner that allowed air to move through the bales of hay. The best way to accomplish this was by creating a line of bodies that would hand off each bale to the next person. We had to do this between the different elevations the hay was to be stacked. After about two hours of tossing the hay bales upwards to the next tier, my arms began to feel like cooked spaghetti, and actually, all the rest of my body as well.

One particular day while stacking hay, I looked down at the next bale making its way toward me and I thought, "I simply don't have the strength." Because I could not appear to be a wimp, I reached for the bale anyway. Now the trick was to use the momentum of the bale of hay itself to fling it up to the next person. Somehow, I managed to fling myself around in a circle clutching the bale of hay as it catapulted me off balance. I fell a few tiers, finally coming to a complete stop. Just then, I felt a sharp stab of pain, I believe in my right ear. Immediately, all I could hear was a very high pitched ringing. It was as if normal sound was now being sucked into a vacuum, with great pressure building in this ear.

The ringing sound was constant, annoying and nerve racking! There was no pain to speak of after the initial puncture occurred. When I fell, a straw of hay slid perfectly into my ear canal, puncturing my eardrum twice. Mr. Johnston, our resident *workaholic* as we called him, hoisted me

29

up like a sack of potatoes and into town we drove. He seemed to know exactly what was needed in that moment. I always thought his name, Johnston, was odd. Everyone I knew was Johnson, so why stick that "t" in there where it simply did not belong?

We drove to the town of Freeville arriving at a single story residence a short time later. The house was white with black trim. Black shutters framed all the windows I could see. The home also served as an office, or had an office attached. The sign in the yard (black with white lettering) read *Doctor of Tympanoplasty*. I was led through the door nearest the sign. I remember looking at that sign and thinking, "doctor of what?"

Once inside, the house did not look at all like a home, but rather a waiting room. I was the only patient. I was led into a room, placed onto a table, and waited. It seemed to me that I waited for hours, ear ringing, and the pressure almost unbearable. I was irritated more than I was curious about what was going to happen next. (I believe this all took place when I was around the age of fourteen.)

Eventually, a very old man entered the room. He slowly walked over to the table shaking like a leaf. (I had no idea what Parkinson's disease was at the time, but this man had to have been suffering from it.) I went from being annoyed to feeling terrified! He began to fidget with the tools he unfurled from a rolled-up cloth. (These tools looked much like dentistry tools, although at that time I don't think I had ever seen a dentist.)

The doctor began to talk to me as he did whatever he was doing. He spoke like I think a grandfather would, kind and reassuring, as he looked into my ear with one of those tools (an otoscope, as it is commonly called). This old man was shaking and unsteady while peeking into my ear. He was telling me to be still, while I was thinking, "You need to be still too!" He announced, "Young man, your ear drum is punctured in two places, but we can fix it!" I watched as he began to explain the procedure. He had a special material, but basically was explaining to me how to patch a bike tire, something I had done many times. The doctor used this analogy to convey to me the ease of what he was about to do.

I laid my head down between what looked like a vise and then the most amazing thing happened, something I have never forgotten to this very day. The moment he picked up the surgical instruments, his shaking completely stopped. He began to do something in my ear with a precision and a confidence I never have forgotten. At one point, the ringing stopped and the pressure subsided instantly. My "inner tube" was patched and all was back to normal.

I share the story because this man was very kind, very nice, and very experienced at his craft. He changed from a feeble, frail old man into superman. More importantly, I began to learn how not to judge appearances as a result of this individual. The Lord used this man and a blade of straw to make a point, so to speak, and he did it so I would hear.

Mrs. Nancy Harris was the art teacher at GJR. I loved art. In the art shop you could do macramé, pottery, sculpting, and painting. You name it, Mrs. Harris taught it. I liked to paint, or at least I did while at GJR.

Ironically, while thumbing through a great big book of photography meant to capture the beauty of Oregon, I found a picture of a mountain lake. I showed it to Mrs. Harris and said, "I think I would like to paint this picture!" "Alright," was her reply! We began to nail the frame together so as to stretch the canvas over the wood. Once that was finished, Mrs. Harris began to explain how to use acrylic paint. I didn't know that oil paint and acrylic paint were different. Actually, I had never even heard the word *acrylic* before.

As soon as I had a basic understanding of paint, it was on to paint brushes. She showed me, over the course of a few days, how different brushes were used to create different effects. I liked the fan brush the most because she could do so many "tricks" with it, as far as painting goes.

Mrs. Harris taught me to draw out the image onto the canvas before using the paint. Soon I was sketching out the lake from the picture book. It was Lost Lake, which is located in Mt Hood National Forest. (I actually have camped there on several occasions.)

The picture hung on the wall of our dining hall, which we called Ewald, named for the relationship the George family had with the Ewald family. I think they all were related by marriage.

My painting, which was a sunset (and quite beautiful), won an award. It was placed on display at a local bank in Freeville, New York, along with other art pieces created by students at GJR. (I never saw my painting after that. Perhaps it was sold; I'm not sure.)

To this day, my art teacher and I are email buddies. She is in her 80's and she is my friend. We somehow found each other a few years ago. Mrs. Harris[1] keeps me connected to GJR in many ways. (From some conversations I have had with her via email, I believe all of us kids whose lives she touched for so many years keep in touch with her as well.)

I learned a great deal as a resident at George Junior Republic. While tucked into those rolling hillsides, I was set apart as a child. Our Lord had wooed me into a church many years earlier, and now He was molding who I was to become.

I left GJR in the fall of 1976, without having a high school diploma. In fact, I ran away. I had achieved various merit positions and excelled in what I was there to do. However, a few of us managed to get marijuana onto the campus and several of us were caught smoking joints. It was during summer vacation, and the campus was mostly empty, except for the kids who had no homes to go to.

I was one of the honorary students who had agreed to forego summer vacation to stay with those who could not leave for any vacation. I was the warden, a position of prestige which took me three years to achieve. The Judge (or Magistrate, as was often the name used inside the court room) and I both were busted. The warden and the judge were off to jail! We were caught with a couple of girls in a compromising position. (Drugs always have a way of causing a "disturbance in the force.") Actually, they can cause chaos in all areas of life.

I was seventeen, in jail (on the campus), and truly humiliated. The embarrassment was too much after having worked so hard to obtain what I had achieved. In all honesty, I punk'd out! This time there was no one else to blame. Back to Rochester I went, but only for a brief time. I never really said goodbye to GJR, and this experience also became part of my identity.

1. Mrs. Harris, a wonderful North Carolina woman, lives both in my memories and my computer. Thanks.

In regard to Don Simkin, on June 29, 2010 while re-reading the manuscript for the billionth time, I sensed the Holy Spirit ask, "Have you tried to contact him?" I searched for his name on the Internet, and found several. I decided to call the first one because of a familiarity with all the particulars that were displayed. Don Simkin answered the phone! Can you believe it? Here I was, nearly 39 years later, speaking to my past.

He was cautious as he listened to me. As I presented more information, he said "Yes, I remember. I remember your mother!" I chuckled to myself, "The *gladiator*!"

We had a wonderful conversation; brief, but wonderful. He asked me to let him know when the book was published. He said he would buy a copy, which afforded me the perfect opportunity to say "Thank you, Mr. Don Simkin; I will send you a copy, free of charge!" (This was a major reason I had called.)

Mr. Simkin is nearly 70 years old. He also expressed kind and affectionate things about GJR during our conversation. I have his address, and now he knows about my appreciation of him all these many years later. (Thank you, Lord, thank you! *At this point, I recommend to young people do not be afraid of facing your mistakes. It truly is the only way to grow. You also will reduce the number of wasted years that inevitably occur when you make the same mistakes over and over again.*)

What was left of our family was living at 107 Elba Street. My two older brothers had left home. I was returning. The afros were fading while the era of disco was at its peak. It was the fall of 1976. Returning home...no rolling hills, no fall colors, nothing of beauty. Mom was tired and so, too, was the life we all had lived. I was different. I was no longer connected to the poverty or the pitiful existence that had followed our family everywhere.

Our dog, Satan, was only a memory, for he had long been dead. That's right, Satan. He was one of the best pets our family had ever known. Satan was a black mutt that one of our uncles had given to us years earlier. One day Satan died after he was hit by a milk truck. He was forever chasing vehicles. (We did not have a vehicle. In fact we didn't have a telephone.) We did not have much when I was growing up. Imagine, losing

Satan was like losing a best friend. How Ironic!

Returning home was wonderful. I love my family; nevertheless, I was different, older. I had seen things, known others from all over New York State, New Jersey and other places. Somehow, I knew I would not be in Rochester for long. One of my younger brothers was getting into all sorts of trouble. I did not see much of him during this time. He eventually was locked up, too. My beautiful brother has been locked up ever since.

There now were seven kids in our family. For the most part, none of us really knew our fathers. We were like most of the kids in the ghetto. The kids who did have fathers didn't want them. Many fathers were drunks, defeated by the color of their skin and the manner in which society had robbed from them. Yet we all were still black and proud. We just didn't know what to be proud of!

That was how it was when I came home. I saw the changes in me in contrast to the people with whom I had grown up. I could not breathe.

Prior to leaving for GJR, shortly after moving to Elba Street, I used to walk down to Jefferson Avenue to where there was a little church constructed from brown stones. I did this on Sunday morning because of my curiosity. I wondered why these very old and frail white people went into this church. I sat outside and listened to them sing. I could hear a man speaking like a teacher. One day, after I had done this for several months, the man saw me sitting outside on the steps.

It was a hot summer morning; the big wooden doors of this little building were open wide. Little did I know at the time, but the Lord was inviting me inside. The man was tall and he wore a long black robe. He stopped speaking as our eyes met. He walked from where he was standing out to where I was sitting, and asked me if I would like to come inside. (I was perhaps eight or nine years old at the time.) I did want to go inside. I was not afraid to do so, and I was glad he had asked. In that moment, this man became another person in my life to thank. *Thank you!* I learned about Jesus that day.

Before I left Rochester in the spring of 1977, I went down to that church. The neighborhood had changed; it was full of black folk and so too, was that church. The sounds that came out of the church were loud

34

and angry. A whole lot of yelling and screaming broke the silence that Sunday morning. The spirit in the church was a different color, and so was the singing.

I was seventeen years old. I loved the black folk of my youth--my friends, my family and especially my home boys. Michael Wall ("Head" as we affectionately called him), if you are still alive, I have loved you most of my life. I still can "hear" you making all of us laugh. Even now, I wonder what happened to so many of my childhood *homies*.

However, in my mind I began to understand something about who I wanted to be. I began to realize I had to escape this place. Something about who I was at seventeen would remain dead if I did not get out of Rochester. I was not trying to escape my youth, but the identity of my youth. Even back then, I wanted to be colorless. I wanted to have my own identity and not the societal lie imposed on so many black people. I didn't want to be *Black and Proud*. As my culture went from the processed look to the dreadlock, the *afro*, the *jeri-curl*, the *braids*, the *fade*, and now the multicolored Miss Clairol look, I began to see a lack of identity driving my culture. I knew there was a God, and I knew I was part of Him.

In Oregon, I met a man who was pouring car oil into his coffee while having dinner at a favorite restaurant in Portland. The restaurant still is there. The building is tired now, old, and it has a number of plumbing problems. (Working as a plumber over the years, I have fixed many things that were falling apart.)

This individual used this oil facade to cause people like me to ask, "Why are you pouring car oil into your coffee?" The year was 1977. I had been in Oregon for a few months (after a Greyhound bus made my escape from Rochester, New York possible that spring). The man's name was Leonard. He explained it actually was honey, and he was a distributor for an oil company. I ended up scheduling a meeting with Leonard; he is very good at drawing people in. Leonard was going to show me the oil business.

The day of the meeting arrived, and I kept my word. My oldest brother came with me. (He had come to Oregon a few years before me.

35

Our father also lived in Oregon.) Leonard told both of us about Jesus. I listened intently to the Gospel message for the first time in a very intimate setting. Leonard was quite intimately open and methodical; he is the consummate sales professional, as well as one of the best Evangelical Christians I have ever known. He was well able to capture my spirit with his words.

I accepted the Lord that night, October 6, 1977. I began to attend Leonard's church. It was full of little frail white people. My friend Leonard is one of those people who brings honor to your whole life. He is an example of the very word *friendship* and he seems to remain a friend for a lifetime.

I also remember attending a Jewish Synagogue somewhere about that same time. A good friend, Rueben (whose last name escapes me), was the son of a very well to do Portland attorney. Going to his home was always an adventure, because the home was full of beautiful relics and artwork of a Jewish nature. Rueben lived in southwest Portland. (I saw his father on several occasions; his mother had died two years before we met.) Rueben was into sports; I think his passion was football. He played for Wilson High School, if memory serves me correctly. I was all of 17 years old, transplanted by my own accord 3,000 miles away from everything I had known, and now I was friends with a Jewish kid.

Most of my childhood friends were Black or Italian; a few Puerto Ricans were part of the ghettos as well. I really never had known anything or anyone Jewish. I do remember several Jewish businesses in my childhood neighborhoods. I thank God for those businesses because they fed us, clothed us, and kept us drunk! I was never one to look upon those Jewish people as taking advantage of the poor folks.

You often hear hate speech against the Jews, but they did for us what a lot of white business owners would not do -- set up shop in the ghetto. Many times Momma would forage through the furniture, coat pockets, and just about everywhere else to find enough money (pocket change, if you will) so that one of the boys could go to the store to get a loaf of bread or some sugar. Many times we simply did not have money to pay, but those Jewish folks would say, "Tell your mother to pay next time," and always with a smile.

Everyone in the neighborhood knew our mother, and almost everyone knew her kids. There were a few Italians, also, who would help us. In those days, you knew all your neighbors, and you knew when things were going bad for them. For example, when the snow was three or four feet high, it was easy to tell who had not paid the Gas & Electric bill because in the evening, no lights were on in the house; often it was ours. (It wasn't so bad in the summertime.)

I was invited to attend a "church" service on Saturday at a Jewish synagogue in Portland. (I was the only black person in the building.) This occurred during the latter part of 1977, shortly before I went into the Navy. Their service was just as weird to me as was most any other religious service I had attended. It seemed to center around a roll of paper on a couple of fancy sticks held by those who carried it. I was clueless as to what was happening. However, the people were extremely nice to me, and accommodating. (I have found this attitude, or personality, of the Jewish people to be the same whenever I have been around them.) Some of the nicest human beings I have known in my life have been Jewish.

More recently, I have attended lectures or events with several Jewish friends who invited me to various events of this nature. One time, early on, a group of Jewish women surrounded me asking things like, "Who do you know?" and/or "Are you here with someone?" I think they were looking to see if I had a detonator or something. I actually quipped, "I am not going to blow up." Smiling, the ladies all laughed, and from that moment forward, I was welcomed. Imagine--living as though everyone wants to kill you!

Anyway, Rueben was a good friend who eventually went on to college. What I remember most is how much he loved his dad! I have since learned an entire history of the Jewish people.

I met a woman who was a survivor of Auschwitz shortly after I entered the world of plumbing and drain cleaning in Portland, Oregon. Out of sheer respect, I wish I could remember her name. This little old Jewish woman changed my life forever. (I did not return to New York after leaving the Navy, as I had fallen in love with the Pacific Northwest and returned there.)

37

I was doing a service in her home related to plumbing. She began to ask if I knew much about the Holocaust. (I did not, outside what was taught in high school. What they teach now is simply repulsive to me.) The lady listened as I answered her questions; she never interrupted my answers. She was kind, sweet, and frail. I began to talk about slavery and the horror inflicted on black people. I had enough knowledge to hold a conversation on the subject, and she listened.

At some point, the lady rolled up her blouse sleeve and revealed to me a series of numbers tattooed into her flesh. As she explained what the numbers meant, I heard the voice of a woman who was strong and resolute in the way she shared the horrible story that was part of her life. Soon I was seated at a table watching an 8 millimeter film of women, little girls, and infant babies being murdered. It is to this day the most horrible thing I have seen on film. It changed my life.

When I left her home, I thought I understood the atrocities committed against the Jewish people. I certainly understood the Holocaust better. I have since learned this sort of thing has happened to the Jews for centuries. In almost every 70 year incremental time period, a "Hitler" has risen up against the Jews.

Unlike what some in Christianity teach, that the Jews killed Christ (which is "rubbish" to quote a very British friend of mine), understanding the following passage in the Holy Scriptures dispels what has been taught for centuries, but one has to study!

Psalms 60:7 (the Tribe of Judah was given a mandate)
"Gilead is mine, and Manasseh is mine; Ephraim also is the strength of my head; Judah is my lawgiver." (There is more in the Bible that reveals much about the suffering of the Jews, but this is for you to go learn about for yourself. While you are at it, learn about who the Lion of the tribe of Judah actually is.)

I began to study about Israel in 1985 or 1986 and never have stopped. The little Jewish woman created in me a desire to know the history, as opposed to having had a snapshot placed into my brain. I began to unravel what I was taught in school, and even go deeper. (All these years later, I am writing this book, and hoping to keep its message very simple.)

These experiences un-colored my mind, for this Jewish lady exposed the capability of my human spirit, once the race issue was nullified. She was not the only person who expedited my leap into the history books. So did Frederick Douglas Junior, Booker T. Washington, Dr. Martin Luther King Junior and, of course, Harriet Tubman. Equally also, did all of the individuals in the Holy scriptures, and even modern day Jews such as Theodor Herzl, Rudolf Vrba, Alfred Weczler, and of course, Zeev Jabotinsky.

In the Navy

In disbelief my shipmates and I watched President Jimmy Carter acquiescing day after day concerning the American hostages being held captive by a bunch of Iranian fanatics who had toppled the government of Muhammad Reza Pahlavi, otherwise known as the Shah of Iran. Here we were, one of the most powerful ships in the Pacific fleet, taking small arms fire from Iranian gun boats in the straits of Hormuz, and we were told to *Stand down!*

The presidential election came and went, but something happened the day Ronald Reagan became president. Not only was it a landslide victory, but we were told to shoot back, and shoot back we did! I sat up and paid attention to the shift in how we were to do things under a Republican versus a Democratic administration. The experience opened a door to study this part of history as well. As a result, I have become "my own mind," so to speak. The color of my skin lost its "Black Power" which, in my opinion, was always a euphemism. I studied the history of both the Democrat and Republican parties. The truth is staring all of us in the face but so, too, is the veil.

If you tell me something that is not true, or if you believe something that simply is not the truth historically, I am quick to address it. In my community, the Black community, I am afforded this opportunity almost daily -- one of many reasons why I am writing this book. Certainly, when it comes to slavery, I can talk about white slavery, Jewish slavery, Indian slavery and African slavery; Human Slavery is the header. None of us has escaped the brutality of slavery, nor have we overcome the sin that promotes it. It was not always a brutal subjugation of one human being over another, but not many in this world can imagine such a time, let alone study the facts of it!

All in all, I have met many people, and loved most of them. This is an intrinsic part of who I am, but also who I choose to be. I am a child of the Kingdom. My experiences are a benefit because of the people who are sharing them with me. Life is like a gigantic Chinese buffet; I keep going back for more. You see, I know how to act around all these people. I feel like one of them, and I thank God for my experiences at George Junior Republic, which taught me to appreciate most of them.

Exodus 24:12

And the Lord said to Moses, Come up to me into the mount, and be there: and I will give you tables of stone, and a law, and commandments which I have written; that you may teach them.

Do you know?

Do you know what the names of the twelve tribes of Israel listed in the book of Revelation reveal?

Genesis 29-35. "Now will I praise the LORD: therefore she called his name Judah.

Genesis 29:32. Reuben: for she said, Surely the LORD hath looked upon my affliction; now therefore my husband will love me.

Genesis 30:11. A troop cometh: and she called his name Gad.

Genesis 3:13. Happy am I, for the daughters will call me blessed: and she called his name Asher.

Genesis 30:8. With great wrestlings have I wrestled with my sister, and I have prevailed: and she called his name Naphtali.

Genesis 41:51. Name of the firstborn Manasseh: For God, said he, hath made me forget all my toil, and my father's entire house.

Genesis 29:33. Because the LORD hath heard I was hated, he hath therefore given me this son also: and she called his name Simeon.

Genesis 29:34. Now this time will my husband be joined unto me, because I have born him three sons: therefore was his name called Levi.

Genesis 30:18. Leah said, God hath given me my hire, because I have given my maiden to my husband: and she called his name Issachar.

Genesis 30:20. God hath endued me with a good dowry; now will my husband dwell with me, because I have born him six sons: and she called his name Zebulun.

Genesis 30:24. She called his name Joseph; and said, The LORD shall add to me another son.

Genesis 30:18. And it came to pass, as her soul was in departing, for she died that she called his name Benoni: but his father called him Benjamin.

When you say the meaning of the names together:

Now will I praise the Lord! Surely the Lord hath looked upon my affliction, a troop cometh. Happy am I, with great wrestling's have I wrestled. For God, said he, hath made me forget all my toil. Because the Lord hath heard I was hated. Now this time will my husband be joined unto me! God hath given me my hire, now will my husband dwell with me. The Lord shall add to me another son. (And it came to pass. A son who sits at the right of the Father.)

Chapter Three:

Jesse

❧•❧   ❧•❧   ❧•❧

Leviticus 22:31

Therefore shall you keep my commandments, and do them: I am the Lord.

❧•❧   ❧•❧   ❧•❧

My father, Jesse, was a lean, dark skinned man. He was full of life, whimsical, and flamboyant. He was a father that none of us wanted. Nevertheless, he was my dad. All of his sons are taller than he was. From my earliest memories of him, he worked! Jesse always had a job.

One particular memory: Early in the morning somewhere in upstate New York, I awoke to the sound of fire engines. My bedroom window was all aglow. I could not have been more than two or three years old at the time. I climbed up to the window (I remember doing this often). My eyes grew wide as I saw what was causing the orange glow. The mill down the way was on fire. As I recall this event from my childhood, it always seems like the biggest thing, a real spectacle. Actually, it was the barn and not the mill, Mom recently told me.

My father worked at the mill. Momma had breakfast on the table for our dad every morning. She already would have made his lunch and placed

43

it into the black lunch pail. I always thought the lunch pail looked like a barn with a handle on the roof. It was long and narrow, black on the outside and white inside. There was a thermos tucked into it. I would not have been surprised if that thermos had been filled with scotch whiskey.

This day was different! I scurried down the stairs only to find chaos. The mood was frantic. Our father was rushing to get out the door. Mom was trying to get my brother ready for school. This was definitely not a normal day.

There was a creek across the street; the road itself was curving off to the left. When turning from that road to go to the mill, one would enter a dirt road that went past our house and Virginia's house. Virginia was a little white girl who lived next door. I think she was a little bit older than me. We often would play "doctor." I think it was because Doctor Kildare always was on the radio inside Virginia's house. (I don't think either of our families had a television set back in those days. I remember now that most radios would light up when they were turned on. If it didn't come on, you had to go to the drug store and buy a tube. Funny thing about those tubes, I knew about them before I knew what a light bulb was!) Anyway, the only two houses on this dirt road to the mill (pathway was more accurate a description) were our house and Virginia's.

On this day, the entire pathway was full of cars and trucks -- fire trucks. I still can remember the heat coming off the inferno that was burning just down the way. I don't remember anything more about the fire or anything else about this house, other than that the bathtub in the incident mentioned earlier about our mother was in this house.

Jesse enjoyed Cadillac cars. When we lived in this house, he had a black Cadillac with a white roof. I don't remember the year (maybe 1957 or 1959) but it was from the fifties. Man, did he love that car! I loved it too. One day I was playing inside his Cadillac. There I was, standing on the seat with this great big steering wheel in my hands. I was having fun! The car was pointed toward the mill. There was a slight hill that took you down to where the mill was located. If you accidentally took the car out of gear, you would start rolling, but not very fast.

So there I was, standing on the seat with this big steering wheel in my hands, rolling down the path. I remember watching my dad run after the car. I did not think he was able to catch me. I was driving pretty fast but my dad was faster. All of a sudden the car door opened, dad jumped in and did something with the stick that was coming out of the steering wheel, and the car stopped. I still can remember my dad holding me under one arm while he walked me back towards the house. He was using his other hand to spank my butt!

I did not know about racism those many years ago. We lived in various places before I was five years old. I clearly can remember only two. White people were always part of those years. It wasn't until we moved to Rochester that I began to see something was not right about people. Our family was never racist; Mom would have none of that sort of behavior. Our father, as best as I can recall, never said a racial thing about anyone. This sort of attitude simply was not a part of my upbringing.

Jesse loved Jazz, too. I still can see him bobbing his head, snapping his fingers to Ella Fitzgerald or Carmen McRae. (He had a particular saying about Carmen McRae; not something to reveal in these pages.) My father had a collection of jazz albums that would stagger the imagination. He had blue records, red records, 33's, 45's, and dozens and dozens of albums. (People find things to worship; we all do. The tribes of the House of Israel had this problem too. I continue to learn how curses move through the generations and the kids always pay the price! My dad worshiped these albums.)

Our father never found his way to worship the King of Glory. He knew the story but rejected the words of the Living God. Jesse enjoyed his brokenness. His issues were not racial but rather sexual. His affections for men and the choices he made as a result left a path of destruction in so many lives, and certainly ours. When I hear people say things like, "Gay people can be happy," or "We're just like everyone else," I think of my father. He was not happy, nor was he like everyone else. My father left a scar on our family as a result of the choices he made that continues to paralyze and humiliate the legacy that was part of how my brothers and I were colored by him.

The words *sins of the father* describe an all too often catch phrase, if you will. However, the lives that spiral out of control as a result continue to cause many problems. To underestimate this is to grow numb to self-destruction. It is this outcome of the chaos we produce by self-destruction that often gets passed along to the next generation. Life is not a lie, but what we hand off to our kids often is.

My father died of various illnesses. He was HIV positive, and cancer had invaded his upper body. I was told Jesse had several tumors up and around his heart muscles. My father drank a fifth of whiskey pretty much daily. His choice of poison was Wild Turkey. I am sure his life was a daily descent into numbness. Near the end, my father was medicated to kill the pain of cancer. Prior to all of this, Jesse was medicated with whiskey to kill the pain of living. I did not attend Jesse's funeral. In the end, he truly was not a part of who I am.

Understanding the way our creator set up creation demands that I know this much about my father if nothing else; he was someone's child too! At one point in his life, something broke inside of him. I watched, participated, and suffered as a result of who and how my dad was.

One day when I was getting ready to leave for the Navy, I visited my father; he was drunk. I asked him the question, "What was it that made you gay?" Jesse told me, "None of your business." From that moment on and for the rest of his life, my father became someone I knew, but he would never be a man I was a part of. While high on cocaine in June 1996, I received the phone call with the message, "Jesse is dead." I hung up on this part of my identity that day.

Like many (not all) in the black community, a father is something other people had. For my dad to buy anything for his biological kids was rare. I was seventeen years old when I saw him again. He was living in Tigard, Oregon with his live-in lover. My father, the homosexual, was facing me, eye to eye. He was not a rotten, lousy man; he was actually fun. I think Jesse put on a show of shows when he was around people. I think this is how he hid the shame of how he lived. Jesse was ashamed, make no mistake about it. Biblically, all of us were affected by the lifestyle he chose. It took many years for most of us to understand the imprinting that occurred as a result of the confusion caused to four sons.

46

I am not sure what a father is; I never had one. Not too long ago, I was thinking about this and it hit me like a brick upside the head! I had no memories, none, of my father ever giving me a present. I do not know what it feels like for a father to hand his child a birthday present (or any present). I have no memory of my father ever coming to my school or buying me clothes; nothing.

One time in Tigard, Oregon on my eighteenth birthday, I was given a surprise birthday party. I never credited my father with having thought of, planned, or been much a part of this party at all, really. He was there; it was held in the home of one of his many friends, but Jesse was like a ghost in my life, whatever that looks like. Janice did this; I know she did it. (I met Janice the day I came to Oregon.) She is famous for this kind of thing. Janice is a former relative by marriage, the mother of my nephew and one of my best friends for thirty-five years. *Thanks Janice!*

On that particular night, the first and only surprise birthday party of my life, if Jesse gave me a gift, I cannot remember it. When I think about the gifts the Lord has given to me and to my life, I can remember almost all of them. He has been my "dad" for the last thirteen years, and we have been developing a rock solid relationship throughout that time.

Funny, sitting here wanting to write about my father, I am somewhat perplexed. I don't know what more there is to write about. I have thought about him more since his death in 1996 than I thought about him when he was alive. I never really wanted to get to know my father.

What I did eventually learn about him was not really worth knowing. He was gay, an alcoholic, and possibly the most pitiful human being I have known. What I think about my father is more on a sad note, rather than an angry one. My relatives within his family are many, and wonderful people. None of us languishes on the failure of Jesse's life. We remember the personality he displayed to us all, and his love for my grandma. My dad was not a bad man, he was a lost man. He remained lost to virtually all his family all his life.

I never have known a homosexual who has had a wonderful life. I have been exposed to many such people as a result of my father and also of being in business. I simply have not seen this as a wonderful, optional life style. Rather, without question, I see broken-ness and a loss of identity. I guess this will be an indelible mark on my life. All the people I know who are gay remind me of my dad, not because of their homosexuality but because I have watched the destruction it causes in the lives of everyone else. Many of these people are caring and thoughtful people. My dad was this way; he just was clueless as to how to accommodate his children.

Homosexuality has been accepted in this day and age, and so, too, are shattered and broken people. However, none of us were created to be shattered and broken. Those who live this way are choosing to live a lie.

If man had crawled out of the ocean a million years ago and fallen in love with another man, mankind would have died off rather quickly. Likewise, if God had made Adam and Adam, none of us would know anything at all because we would not be here.

I have learned that a lie is something that is added to the truth. This seems to be acceptable to those who are shattered, regardless of a person's sexual identity.

Jesse fathered five children; all of us were broken the day we were born and so, too, was our mother. Imagine for a moment the hope that drained out of her spirit because of the choices my father made.

We have tools we use against one another that shatter and break us. My father was full of life; but I think, and will continue to think, that he really hated every minute of it.

Rabbi Shaul, aka Apostle Paul

The Apostle Paul (Rabbi Shaul) was not given a new identity alone, but a restored truth as well. He was delivering the Torah to the Gentiles. He was not creating a Christian congregation, he was leading people back to the concepts found in the Torah. The Lord is, and always has been, the goal of the Law. He is its Commandments, Statutes, and Law and so in hearing and doing them, we are led to Him and to safety in Him. His blood was shed for the redemption and restoration of Israel, and all those grafted in and adopted by the groom, Yeshua. He is unlimited, and so is His word.

Without acknowledging the renewing of the covenant made with Judah and Israel (Jeremiah 31:31-40 and Hebrews 10:15-25), one cannot participate in salvation. The entire word of the Lord is very clear concerning this. The Jews are not excluded. Torah was presented to all of Christianity through those who took the *Besorah* of Rabbi Shaul to the nations as part of the renewing and coming restoration of the two kingdoms of Israel--Judah and Ephraim. Regardless of the corruption found in both, the plan continues and both need to come together as one.

Torah & the Gospel (or Besorah) are one plan, not two!

Matthew 15:24 "But he answered and said, I am not sent but to the lost sheep of the house of Israel"

Ezekiel 34:12 "As a shepherd seeks out his flock in the day that he is among his sheep that are scattered, so will I seek out my sheep, and will deliver them out of all places where they have been scattered in the cloudy and dark day."

James 1:1 "James, a servant of God and of the Lord Jesus Christ, to the twelve tribes which are scattered abroad, greeting."

1 Peter 1:1 "Peter, an apostle of Jesus Christ, To God's elect, strangers in the world, scattered throughout Pontus, Galatia, Cappadocia, Asia and Bithynia,"

(Paul knew the Torah and taught it to everyone, just as did our Messiah; Jesus never pulled out the letters and testimonies of the New Testament to teach of them, did he?) I have listed several verses of scripture that show how often Paul quoted the books of Moses.

Romans 2:11 "For there is no respect of persons with God."

Deuteronomy 10:17 "For the Lord your God is God of gods, and Lord of lords, a great God, a mighty, and a terrible, which regards not persons, nor takes reward"

Romans 4:3 "For what said the scripture? Abraham believed God, and it was counted to him for righteousness."

Genesis 15:6 "And he believed in the Lord; and he counted it to him for righteousness."

Romans 4:17 "(as it is written, I have made you a father of many nations [a]) in the presence of Him whom he believed—God, who gives life to the dead and calls those things which do not exist as though they did."

Genesis 17:5 "Neither shall your name any more be called Abram, but your name shall be Abraham; for a father of many nations have I made you."

Romans 7:7 "What shall we say then? Is the law sin? God forbid. No, I had not known sin, but by the law: for I had not known lust, except the law had said, You shall not covet."

Exodus 20:17 "You shall not covet your neighbor's house, you shall not covet your neighbor's wife, nor his manservant, nor his maidservant, nor his ox, nor his ass, nor any thing that is your neighbor's."

Deuteronomy 5:21 "Neither shall you desire your neighbor's wife, neither shall you covet your neighbor's house, his field, or his manservant, or his maidservant, his ox, or his ass, or any thing that is your neighbor's."

Genesis 12:12 "And God said to Abraham, Let it not be grievous in your sight because of the lad, and because of your female slave; in all that Sarah has said to you, listen to her voice; for in Isaac shall your seed be called."

Romans 9:15 "For he said to Moses, I will have mercy on whom I will have mercy, and I will have compassion on whom I will have compassion."

Exodus 33:19 "And he said, I will make all my goodness pass before you, and I will proclaim the name of the Lord before you; and will be gracious to whom I will be gracious, and will show mercy on whom I will show mercy."

Romans 9:17 "For the scripture said to Pharaoh, Even for this same purpose have I raised you up, that I might show my power in you, and that my name might be declared throughout all the earth."

Exodus 9:16 "And in very deed for this cause have I raised you up, for to show in you my power; and that my name may be declared throughout all the earth."

Romans 10:5 "For Moses describes the righteousness which is of the law, That the man which does those things shall live by them."

Leviticus 18:5 "You shall therefore keep my statutes, and my judgments: which if a man do, he shall live in them: I am the Lord."

Romans 10:6 "But the righteousness which is of faith speaks on this wise, Say not in your heart, Who shall ascend into heaven? (that is, to bring Christ down from above)."

Deuteronomy 30:12 "It is not in heaven, that you should say, Who shall go up for us to heaven, and bring it to us, that we may hear it, and do it?"

Romans 10:8 "But what said it? The word is near you, even in your mouth, and in your heart: that is, the word of faith, which we preach."

Deuteronomy 30:14 "But the word is very near to you, in your mouth, and in your heart, that you may do it."

Deuteronomy 32:21 "They have moved me to jealousy with that which is not God; they have provoked me to anger with their vanities: and I will move them to jealousy with those which are not a people; I will provoke them to anger with a foolish nation."

Romans 12:19 "Dearly beloved, avenge not yourselves, but rather give place to wrath: for it is written, Vengeance is mine; I will repay, said the Lord."

Deuteronomy 32:35 "To me belongs vengeance and recompense; their foot shall slide in due time: for the day of their calamity is at hand, and the things that shall come on them make haste."

Romans 13:9 "For this, You shall not commit adultery, You shall not kill, You shall not steal, You shall not bear false witness, You shall not covet; and if there be any other commandment, it is briefly comprehended in this saying, namely, You shall love your neighbor as yourself."

Exodus 20:13 "You shall not kill."

Romans 15:10 "And again he said, Rejoice, you Gentiles, with HIS people."

Deuteronomy 32:43 "Rejoice, O you nations, with HIS people: for he will avenge the blood of HIS servants, and will render vengeance to his adversaries, and will be merciful to HIS land, and to HIS people."

Galatians 2:6 "But of these who seemed to be somewhat, (whatever they were, it makes no matter to me: God accepts no man's person) for they who seemed to be somewhat in conference added nothing to me."

Deuteronomy 10:17 "For the Lord your God is God of gods, and Lord of lords, a great God, a mighty, and a terrible, which regards not persons, nor takes reward."

Galatians 3:6 "Even as Abraham believed God, and it was accounted to him for righteousness."

Genesis 15:6 "And he believed in the Lord; and he counted it to him for righteousness."

Galatians 3:8 "And the scripture, foreseeing that God would justify the heathen through faith, preached before the gospel to Abraham, saying, in you shall all nations be blessed."

Genesis 22:18 "And in your seed shall all the nations of the earth be blessed; because you have obeyed my voice."

Galatians 3:10 "For as many as are of the works of the law are under the curse: for it is written, Cursed is every one that continues not in all things which are written in the book of the law to do them."

Deuteronomy 27:26 "Cursed be he that confirms not all the words of this law to do them. And all the people shall say, Amen."

Galatians 3:12 "And the law is not of faith: but, the man that does them shall live in them."

Leviticus 18:5 "You shall therefore keep my statutes, and my judgments: which if a man do, he shall live in them: I am the Lord."

Galatians 3:13 "Christ has redeemed us from the curse of the law, being made a curse for us: for it is written, Cursed is every one that hangs on a tree."

Deuteronomy 21:23 "His body shall not remain all night on the tree, but you shall in any wise bury him that day; (for he that is hanged is accursed of God;) that your land be not defiled, which the Lord your God gives you for an inheritance." (He perfected the law, he did not fulfill it as Christianity teaches.)

Galatians 3:16 "Now to Abraham and his seed were the promises made. He said not, And to seeds, as of many; but as of one, And to your seed, which is Christ." (Yeshua)

Genesis 22:18 "And in your seed shall all the nations of the earth be blessed; because you have obeyed my voice."

Galatians 3:17 "And this I say, that the covenant, that was confirmed before of God in Christ, the law, which was four hundred and thirty years after, cannot cancel, that it should make the promise of none effect."

Exodus 12:40 "Now the sojourning of the children of Israel, who dwelled in Egypt, was four hundred and thirty years."

Galatians 4:22 "For it is written, that Abraham had two sons, the one by a female slave, the other by a free woman."

Genesis 21:2 "For Sarah conceived, and bare Abraham a son in his old age, at the set time of which God had spoken to him."

AND Genesis 21:9 "And Sarah saw the son of Hagar the Egyptian, which she had born to Abraham, mocking."

Galatians 4:22 "For it is written, that Abraham had two sons, the one by a female slave, the other by a free woman."

Genesis 16:15 "And Hagar bore Abram a son: and Abram called his son's name, which Hagar bore, Ishmael."

Galatians 4:30 "Nevertheless what said the scripture? Cast out the female slave and her son: for the son of the female slave shall not be heir with the son of the free woman."

Genesis 21:10 "Why she said to Abraham, Cast out this female slave and her son: for the son of this female slave shall not be heir with my son, even with Isaac."

Galatians 5:14 "For all the law is fulfilled in one word, even in this; You shall love your neighbor as yourself."

Leviticus 19:18 "You shall not avenge, nor bear any grudge against the children of your people, but you shall love your neighbor as yourself: I am the LORD."

Colossians 2:11 "In whom also you are circumcised with the circumcision made without hands, in putting off the body of the sins of the flesh by the circumcision of Christ."

Deuteronomy 10:16 "Circumcise therefore the foreskin of your heart, and be no more stiff necked."

Colossians 3:25 "But he that does wrong shall receive for the wrong which he has done: and there is no respect of persons."

Deuteronomy 10:17 "For the Lord your God is God of gods, and Lord of lords, a great God, a mighty, and a terrible, which regards not persons, nor takes reward."

These scriptures are only a very few when compared to all that Paul quoted. (Remember, Rabbi Shaul was a Pharisee until the day of his death.)

On the road to Damascus, if I was brought to my knees as a black man by the Lord but stood up as a white man, it would be more suitable in my understanding for Rabbi Shaul to stand up a Christian. However, he never stopped going to the Temple, he obeyed the Sabbath and the Festivals, and he taught the books of Moses (who was given this information face to face with the Lord). Remember, the New Testament did not exist thus Rabbir Paul was restored to the Torah and it's proper context by Yeshua Himself (who also never quoted the New Testament). Paul, like Moses to the Hebrew's took God's instruction to the Gentile.

Remember, the Lord wrote this down with his finger on two stone tablets. He spoke the oral Torah to Moses face to face. He spoke the oral Torah for the Jews. However, most don't know the difference.

I encourage you to study. The seven churches were teaching Torah. All were placed in Asia Minor (those mentioned in Revelation), the Living word of the Lion went forth, and Rabbi Paul wrote several letters to the Gentiles confirming the continuation of his purpose.

> The conversion of Paul was that the living word, Torah, was restored to him. He began to follow a Jewish Rabbi who, approximately 25 years earlier, died and rose again.

Below are links to Pastor Mark Biltz' (El Shaddai Ministries) teaching concerning Rabbi Shaul[1] or Paul.[2]

---

1. *Paul, the Mystery Man*, (http://elshaddaiministries.us/audio/hayesod/20070827h9.html). Part 9: A study on Saul of Tarsus, the Torah teacher par excellence.

2. *Paul, the Misunderstood Man*, (http://elshaddaiministries.us/audio/hayesod/20070903h10.html). Part 10: Rethinking many of the common misunderstanding that has been fostered concerning Paul's teachings about the Torah.

Chapter Four:

Cocaine

Deuteronomy 5:10

And showing mercy to thousands of them that love me and keep my commandments...

I received the call in the early afternoon. One of my friend's kids was found dead in the crib! This was some time ago in the early 1990's.

The little girl had somehow managed to unravel the satin border around her baby blanket, becoming entangled with this strip wrapped around her neck and suffocated, or hung herself. It was a heartbreaking moment. Losing a child is awful. None of the people I called friends were ready to hear this news. All of us were serving ourselves. For a brief moment, we had to deal with life through the death of this little girl. The funeral was full of weeping friends and relatives. I remember looking at the older brother. He was maybe 3 years old. He really had no idea what was occurring, and he had only known his little sister for less than 12 months. His family was torn apart over this incident. He was growing into a world full of loss.

After the funeral, several of us went to a gathering for the family. I happened to stumble into a room where some of the attendees were smoking marijuana. I had pretty much given up on getting high with pot. I was a bit worn out on hacking until I had a headache, eating until I was bloated, and being brain dead from the rest of the effects of smoking marijuana! I was no stranger to drugs, and had done my share. I was not serving the Lord at all during this time in my life. The world tosses you a treat disguised as something exotic or curious. On this day, I was given a pipe full of dynamite and it blew my world to hell. I saw a young woman sitting on a sofa doing something with cocaine that I had not seen before. Without providing the details of what she was doing, suffice it to say I was introduced to crack cocaine.

I think that the very first toke from the glass pipe handed to me indoctrinated me into what would become the worst time of my adult life. I became addicted to this drug that day. I remember this very young woman asking, "Do you want to try this?" She added that it would not burn your nose like snorting it does, a selling point I suppose. This one moment in time turned into several years of the most self-destructive, emotionally bankrupt time of my life. I have the evidence to prove it. My marriage really never recovered from this, and my kids suffered terribly during their formative years as a result. All of our lives fell into a deep hole that day. The father of the family (that would be me) was abusing his world and everything within it. Self-destruction of the human spirit is easily transferred to the demons for blame when we stop accepting responsibility for what has been given us. I blamed myself; that was the problem. Accepting responsibility for hating yourself...is very hard to do!

Soon after the introduction to crack cocaine, the mother of the little girl died while riding in a helicopter. The helicopter rides were part of the entertainment at a company picnic. Of course, by then her marriage had failed, and all her friends were crack cocaine addicts. Prior to these events, the mother of the little girl had been the Maid of Honor at my wedding a few years earlier. Her remaining son was now fully engulfed in trauma. I was a fool, and people whom I loved were dying.

Drugs are the quickest, most effective way to lose everything. The plans working against you are diabolic; you cannot win. I should have known better, but no one ever taught me to know better about drugs. I was taught how to do what I was told; everyone used drugs. Nevertheless, getting high became as necessary as was being employed. I was spending huge amounts of money to secure this drug while at the same time trying to maintain a marriage that was a dysfunctional nightmare. The obscenity of drugs, or any addiction, is that while it is busy destroying everything, we chase it down the street throwing money at it. We also throw the DVD player, cameras, camcorders, cars, anything worth anything, including the presents you purchase for your children, down the street too. Meanwhile personal integrity, self respect, and everything in between is being shredded in front of the whole world. My world was my children.

The more you delve into this form of idolatry, the more you grow to hate yourself. The more you hate yourself, the more you chase the addiction down the street. As I have said, drug addiction is diabolical. All addictions must have the same DNA, because the end game is chaos. We teach our children, handing it down if you will, how to exist in chaos. I was acting out my own colorful childhood *vis a vis* the lives of my own family. I lost everything. Throughout all of this, the one thing I did not lose was my wife; part of her pain came with the ring. I never got beyond her pain. However dysfunctional we were, I loved the woman I married; don't misunderstand how I mean what I have shared about us.

Taking care of my family and raising four kids was a monumental undertaking. I had to deal with a sort of pressure that is impossible to manage. In truth, I was out of control and life was crashing all around me.

I stood before a few Judges several years later wondering how in the world I allowed this. The childhood memories of the Monroe County Juvenile Detention Facility never entered my thoughts. These events were all grown-up, and I had to own up to the damage my drug abuse caused to everyone. Virtually all of my courtroom exhibitions were the result of bad business decisions; white collar stupidity, if you will. As I think about the path of destruction I personally led my family through, I thank God for not tossing me under the bus. He kept hope alive.

One day my oldest son handed me my crack pipe and asked, "What is this, dad?" This memory has been seared into my brain ever since. I think he was about twelve years old at the time.

59

I would go to church on Sunday and be high as a kite by 5:00 p.m. that day. My kids would be sitting in the pews while I was worshiping the Lord, and in between thinking about when I would be able to get some more cocaine! This nightmare went on for several insidious years.

My kids now are transitioning from the teenage years to the young adult years. They have each struggled with years of anger and hostility. My family was broken many years ago. My wife was broken long before I knew her. Traveling down the road of addiction affected everyone in my family. We all were hurt because of it. Believe me when I say to you the consequences of drug abuse are devastating. I accept fully and completely my contributions to my now failed marriage. The love of my life needed a much stronger man than I was able to be.

One day in February 1998, I walked out into the living room of a very empty and lonely apartment, fell on my knees and cried out to the Lord, "Please stop this drug abuse and addiction!" Two days later, a church van broadsided me while I was accidentally running a red light. I don't remember the impact, but I do remember waking up in the ambulance. I was wondering "When did I come home and go to bed in order to be having this dream?" It was all surreal. The medical personnel were doing all sorts of things to me; the mood was frantic. Meanwhile, I was thinking, "Wow, I have to wake up from this dream!"

The Emergency Medical Technician (EMT) was yelling, "You have been in a serious automobile accident. We are transporting you to the trauma center." The accident was very bad; I am thankful to have survived it. The one EMT stuck me with an IV needle, and the dream ended in that moment. I felt the prick of the needle and instantly knew this was really happening! I started trying to get out of there. Then I felt another needle prick as I was fighting off the EMT (He knew just what to do with people like me.) Sometime later I woke up in an emergency room hospital bed, with all sorts of things connected to me.

The doctors were talking about the swelling of my heart. It seems to me as I attempt to remember the events of this night they were talking about putting ice into my chest. How on earth were they going to do that? (Even to this day I wonder if the swelling of my heart was the result of the crack cocaine rather than the car accident.) I was drifting in and out of consciousness. When next I became aware of my surroundings, the words were somewhat more encouraging. They were discussing how my heart had returned to a normal rhythm. My wife was in the room. I began to toss everything I could physically grab with my hands at her. The doctors asked her to leave.

I ran that red light because I was distracted; my mind was a million miles removed from physically driving a car. This still remains bizarre to me. All of a sudden the interior of the car lit up. I was driving a 1994 Ford Escort, the type that had the automatic seatbelts that strapped you in as soon as you turned the key. (More like strangled you as I remember.) I just had left my son's basketball game and was headed to a business meeting. I was so angry at what I had just witnessed that my thoughts were immersed in rage! (I think we all have moments of rage that border insanity. This was one of those moments for me.)

The interior of the car became very bright and I regained a split second of consciousness from the rage coursing through my entire being, only to see in that instant a red light that I was just passing under. I looked to my left and saw a headlight a foot or two away from my face. It was just after 7:00 p.m. The sun had gone down; there was no light other than passing traffic. The church van was going about its merry old way when all of a sudden I became the deer in the headlights. The impact occurred at about 40 MPH. To this day, I don't know the driver of the other vehicle.

When I came home from the hospital a few days later, I went to jail. I was wrapped up in all manner of bandages. I had a few cracked ribs and stitches in my head, and now I was sitting in a jail cell, wondering why. I was separated from my family at the time all this was happening. My little apartment, where a week or so earlier I had dropped down to my knees, asking "Stop this madness, please Lord" had been exchanged for a jail cell. "How do I get high in here?" I remembered thinking. I was in jail for a couple of days. The judge let me out on Monday.

During that week, I did get high on crack cocaine but I went to church the following Sunday. A friend brought me home. I invited him in for coffee. Before the coffee was done brewing, a loud pounding began at my apartment door. I asked, "Who is it?" The reply was, "The Police. Please

61

open the door." I opened the door to find about 15 police officers, guns drawn. My friend quite possibly went into shock. He was an older gentleman who certainly was not prepared for what was happening. It seemed that the district attorney did not like the fact that the Judge had released me earlier in the week. In fact, the police did not know why they were there to arrest me. I was handcuffed and taken to a local precinct so they could find out why I was being arrested. (Go figure!)

My wife had made an accusation that simply was not true. Nevertheless, I spent fourteen days behind bars. The Lord was stopping me. (I had not made the connection to all these bizarre events, but the Lord kept taking me out of that apartment.)

Obviously, there is a great deal more to speak about concerning this period in time, but what is important to realize is that the Lord was answering my prayer when I had asked Him to stop the madness.

In March of 1998, I began to have a headache. The intensity of the headache pain seemed to increase daily, until I was literally bed-ridden and afraid to even move a muscle! The pain was excruciating. Actually, it was beyond excruciating. I was eating every medication I could get my hands on--Tylenol, Aleve, Aspirin; you name it, I was taking it. Nothing seemed to have any effect whatsoever. For two weeks I lay in my bed, not eating very much and literally afraid to move.

I finally went to the doctor and explained this headache was now two weeks old. My doctor suggested I was having a migraine, possibly from the car accident in February. He administered a butt shot and sent me home. He told me to come back if the shot did not help. I slept very little, and the next morning when I opened my eyes (which was painful to do), everything looked as though I was inches away from a fluorescent light. Had the shot made me blind? I could not see anything except this brightness. I felt my way to the living room, thinking this would pass and my sight would adjust. This did not happen. I was near panic, with a migraine exploding in my head. I dropped to my knees and screamed out to the Lord, "Lord, what now?"

My friend Randy was at my home within five minutes. (Randy is the father of my oldest son's childhood friend Zack. Zack always puts a smile

62

on my face whenever I think about him. He occupies one of those places in my heart.) Anyway, off to see the doctor.

The doctor suggested I have another "CAT" scan to see if something else was going on inside my head and I was whisked off to another part of the hospital. When I returned an hour or two later, my wife was present and Randy, I believe, was gone. My wife looked as if she had seen a ghost. My eyesight was much better, but everything was blurry or out of focus. The brightness had faded, but something was surely wrong; I could feel it.

The nurse was connecting me into an IV unit (or so I thought), stating this would help with the migraine. (He actually was the anesthesiologist and was knocking me out, but no one told me that little detail.) My wife had told them I would jump off that table and run for the doors if I knew they were about to open up my head. I was rushed into surgery with a sub-epidural hematoma (bleeding in the brain). The fact that this bleeding had been occurring for over two weeks was astonishing. Even more amazing, according to the doctor, was the fact that I was alive at all. They were not sure I would survive the surgery.

I awoke the next morning to find three neurosurgeons standing around my bed. As I surveyed the surrounding room, they were surveying me. My doctor was among those in the room. He asked my name to which I answered, "Jeff." They all looked at one another as if I had just won a prize!

Another doctor asked the next question, "Who is the president of the United States of America?" I said, "Please don't tell me Hilary Clinton." They chuckled. These doctors were amazed that I was cognitive at all. I would eventually find out that I was a miracle and they were trying to determine why.

My mother flew out from New York; she was there in the hospital when I awoke. Mom had been staying at my apartment. When I returned home, the entire apartment was spotless. It looked like a home. While living alone with the demons of cocaine, the brokenness of the separation from my children, being a drug addict, and all the misery I wallowed in was gone. I stood at the door of my apartment almost afraid to enter. In that moment, all the strife and bitterness that had existed between my mother

63

and me evaporated. Mom has become a very good friend, and I cherish every moment I have with her. (Currently our relationship is carried on over the telephone, but that phone connects my heart to hers for sure.)

That day, I was fearful of going back into the life I had been living. However, that day was the day the Lord delivered me from cocaine. I never have relapsed nor used drugs of any kind since that day. Little did I know at the time that my very Christian mother, while I was in the hospital fighting to live, had chased away the spirits of hell that had held me captive to cocaine. Mom cleaned up my home in more ways than one might think. Along with the God of Israel doing battle on my behalf, so was my mom!

The surgery happened on April 1 (April Fool's Day). Our God has a fabulous sense of humor! I remember my beloved mother-in-law saying to me one day, "You're not such a bad guy now that they fixed your brain." I loved my mother-in-law, even though she was the kookiest, most miserable woman I had come to know while I was living in the Pacific Northwest. Clara was German. She came to America after World War II as a newly married wife of a US Army soldier. He was her ticket to leave the hell of Germany behind. It took her forty years to return to Germany. Clara died of Alzheimer's disease in October of 2004. Clara helped me more than any other live human being to get my life turned around and back on track toward becoming the person God created me to be. I wish to express something to Mrs. Clara B. *Thank you!*

Every addict comes in a variety of colors

(This is the existential truth about addiction in and of itself.)

When I sat down to write this book, I knew that I would write about this period of my life. I do so not as a moment of accomplishment, but rather recognizing that I was allowed to overcome a nightmare. Far too many of us die. I am sharing this because it is part of my life and because it also is when my life began to turn around. Even in this, I had to *Un-Color* myself from being the most worthless human being I knew.

Hope is just that; hope. All of us have it, all of us know of it. I remember quite clearly sitting on the edge of my bed shortly after being delivered from crack cocaine. The room began to fill with an evil that was nearly suffocating. I thought I was having a panic attack. It was as if I could cut the air in the room with a knife!

There I was, sitting on the edge of the bed, when I heard a voice -- a very dark, calculating voice -- say to me, "So you're going to start praying to God, huh? Well, watch out what you pray for!" I turned my head to see what had just spoken to me and nothing was there. I was reminded in that moment that we are in a battle. I had won and this voice was not happy about it! It was nice to know that something spiritually bankrupt had lost a stronghold in my life. I had hope, and this voice knew it.

The Lord completely and utterly destroyed the tentacles of drug addiction and drug use that was rooted deeply into so many years of my life. I often reflect back with even more appreciation to the Lord for what he did for me. I feel myself and I feel connected to the very reason I was created. No cigarettes, no drugs of any kind, and no self-destructive behavior dictating to me how to get through another day.

I remember the day I walked out into my living room, fell to my knees, and asked the Lord to stop me. He hit me with a church van and has had my attention ever since. Cast off the lie that makes you feel less than "The Greatest Story Ever Told!" The ability to do this is how we are able to do anything. We are the *Un-Colored* Kids of the Kingdom -- not drug addicts.

For the record, I still love my wife very much. One day I pray that she will walk into her living room, drop to her knees, and ask the Lion of the tribe of Judah to help her. We all need to do this, no matter how together we think we are. The mother of my kids is not a bad person.

The spiritual battle that occurs in all our lives is relentless. Now that I am intimately connected to the heroes of the bible and see the story from a Hebraic perspective, I am able to relate to the personal difficulties of Moses and Aaron. Joshua lived a life of death and destruction. He led the children of a people into war and heartache. Even Queen Esther lived assimilated and undercover while a madman was trying to kill millions of her countrymen.

These people overcame much adversity. They are a stalwart connection to who we are. We all are of these people, and the Lord is revealing himself through us, just as he did on virtually every page of the lives of these folks. Learning about the Hebrew nature of our Messiah has built a fortified wall that cannot be overtaken between me and the lie of drug abuse. The bible is alive and illuminated in a way that simply staggers my senses. Cocaine is a lie, methamphetamines are a lie, and alcoholism is a lie. If you are under the influence of any such substances, then you have been robbed.

As you continue reading *Un-Coloring Race*, the person who stares back at you in the mirror is not a stranger. That person is not the problem. That person has a purpose. The world was not created in order to accommodate accidental births. If you have not felt worthy, it is because you have forgotten how, or may never have known how to do so. You were born worthy; this too is intrinsic. So much so, that the God of creation knows your name. He does not know you because of failure, but rather because of love – unconditional love. If you need to snap out of something that has you bound, it is your choice to do so.

Father, I thank you for delivering me from the lie of drug abuse. Thank you for getting rid of the insects that were carrying me to destruction. Thank you because I, too, snapped out of it!

If you struggle with drug addiction or any addiction that is destroying who you are, I encourage you to get help. Ask someone to help you, and even better, ask the Creator of everything that you know to help you to know him. Send me an email... but do something else, anything else, to change the path you have been on.

Chapter Five:
Contemplate a Mental Shift

I Kings 6:12

Concerning this house which you are building, if you will walk in My statutes, and execute My judgments, and keep all My commandments to walk in them; then will I perform My word with you, which I spoke to David your father.

Imagine you're sitting in a room full of people who have a completely different culture, language, and identity. They represent people who are so vastly unfamiliar to all your sensibilities that it simply feels odd, and strangely uncomfortable to you. Nevertheless, these are the people with which God made an everlasting covenant.

Genesis 17:7-8

"And I will establish My covenant between Me and you and your descendants after you in their generations, for an everlasting covenant, to be God to you and your descendants after you. Also I give to you and your descendants after you the land in which you are a stranger, all the land of Canaan, as an everlasting possession; and I will be their God."

You pull out a copy of the New Testament and begin to read quietly to yourself from the book of John. You know these people are the very people that Joshua led into the promised land. You have a relationship with these people, but centuries of change exists between you and them. These people are the children of those who came out of Egypt. It is these very children who were trained up in the way that a child should go. They are the finished product of a freed people who were taught the first five books of Moses, or the instructions given by Yeshua. These are the people who would become the Nation of Israel, or the Kingdom Kids named after Jacob (whose name was changed to Israel).

Genesis 35:10

"And God said to him, Your name is Jacob: your name shall not be called any more Jacob, but Israel shall be your name: and he called his name Israel."

They were taught about the Lord, learning of Yeshua's Festivals/ Feasts or Holy Days (holidays, if using the watered down version). These days that he so carefully imprinted into this nation are His days; they never belonged to Israel, and certainly were not for the Jews alone. This nation was to take who He was and is, Torah, to the rest of the nations of the world.

Leviticus 23:1-22

The Feasts

[1-2]And the Lord spoke to Moses, saying, Speak to the children of Israel, and say to them: The feasts of the Lord, which you shall proclaim to be holy convocations, These are My feasts.

The Sabbath

[3]Six days shall work be done, but the seventh day is a Sabbath of solemn rest, a holy convocation. You shall do no work on it; it is the Sabbath of the Lord in all your dwellings.

The Passover and Unleavened Bread

[4]These are the feasts of the Lord, holy convocations which you shall proclaim at their appointed times. [5]On the fourteenth day of the first month at twilight is the Lord's Passover. [6]And on the fifteenth day of the same month is the Feast of Unleavened Bread to the Lord; seven days you must eat

unleavened bread. [7]On the first day you shall have a holy convocation; you shall do no customary work on it. [8]But you shall offer an offering made by fire to the Lord for seven days. The seventh day shall be a holy convocation; you shall do no customary work on it.

The Feast of First Fruits

[9]And the Lord spoke to Moses, saying, [10]"Speak to the children of Israel, and say to them: 'When you come into the land which I give to you, and reap its harvest, then you shall bring a sheaf of the first fruits of your harvest to the priest. [11]He shall wave the sheaf before the Lord, to be accepted on your behalf; on the day after the Sabbath the priest shall wave it. [12]And you shall offer on that day, when you wave the sheaf, a male lamb of the first year, without blemish, as a burnt offering to the Lord. [13]Its grain offering shall be two-tenths of an ephah of fine flour mixed with oil, an offering made by fire to the Lord, for a sweet aroma; and its drink offering shall be of wine, one-fourth of a hin. [14]You shall eat neither bread nor parched grain nor fresh grain until the same day that you have brought an offering to your God; it shall be a statute forever throughout your generations in all your dwellings.'

The Feast of Weeks

[15]'And you shall count for yourselves from the day after the Sabbath, from the day that you brought the sheaf of the wave offering: seven Sabbaths shall be completed. [16]Count fifty days to the day after the seventh Sabbath; then you shall offer a new grain offering to the Lord. [17]You shall bring from your dwellings two wave loaves of two-tenths of an ephah. They shall be of fine flour; they shall be baked with leaven. They are the first fruits to the Lord. [18]And you shall offer with the bread seven lambs of the first year, without blemish, one young bull, and two rams. They shall be as a burnt offering to the Lord, with their grain offering and their drink offerings, an offering made by fire for a sweet aroma to the Lord. [19]Then you shall sacrifice one kid of the goats as a sin offering, and two male lambs of the first year as a sacrifice of a peace offering. [20]The priest shall wave them with the bread of the first fruits as a wave offering before the Lord, with the two lambs. They shall be holy to the Lord for the priest. [21]And you shall proclaim on the same day that it is a holy convocation to you. You shall do no customary work on it. It shall be a statute forever in all your dwellings throughout your generations. [22]When you reap the harvest of your land, you shall not wholly reap the corners of your field when you reap, nor shall you

69

gather any gleaning from your harvest. You shall leave them for the poor and for the stranger: I am the Lord your God.'"

The Israelites were taught to understand his calendar and appointed times, which are the feast days. He began to tell Moses and Aaron to record prophetic appointments whereby he would intersect humanity based on his Holy days, his Festivals. The Lord wanted us to be joyous when he came to us; he wanted to throw a party. Certain feasts were pilgrimages to Jerusalem. The Father wanted everyone present when his son was born of flesh. Such was the case when He was born on the Feast of Tabernacles, "God is with us!"

Exodus 12:1-14

[1]Now the LORD spoke to Moses and Aaron in the land of Egypt, saying, [2]"This month shall be your beginning of months; it shall be the first month of the year to you. [3]Speak to all the congregation of Israel, saying: 'On the tenth of this month every man shall take for himself a lamb, according to the house of his father, a lamb for a household. [4]And if the household is too small for the lamb, let him and his neighbor next to his house take it according to the number of the persons; according to each man's need you shall make your count for the lamb. [5]Your lamb shall be without blemish, a male of the first year. You may take it from the sheep or from the goats. [6]Now you shall keep it until the fourteenth day of the same month. Then the whole assembly of the congregation of Israel shall kill it at twilight. [7]And they shall take some of the blood and put it on the two doorposts and on the lintel of the houses where they eat it. [8]Then they shall eat the flesh on that night; roasted in fire, with unleavened bread and with bitter herbs they shall eat it. [9]Do not eat it raw, nor boiled at all with water, but roasted in fire—its head with its legs and its entrails. [10]You shall let none of it remain until morning, and what remains of it until morning you shall burn with fire. [11]And thus you shall eat it: with a belt on your waist, your sandals on your feet, and your staff in your hand. So you shall eat it in haste. It is the Lord's **Passover**. [12]For I will pass through the land of Egypt on that night, and will strike all the firstborn in the land of Egypt, both man and beast; and against all the gods of Egypt I will execute judgment: I am the Lord. [13]Now the blood shall be a sign for you on the houses where you are. And when I see the blood, I will pass over you; and the plague shall not be on you to destroy you when I strike the land of Egypt. [14]So this day shall be to you as a memorial; and you

shall keep it as a feast to the Lord throughout your generations. You shall keep it as a feast by an everlasting ordinance.'"

They are the children that learned how to worship the living God while being raised up in a desert journey. These are the children who witnessed the death of their parents in the wilderness. Many are the descendants of the sons of Jacob but others are Egyptians who left with most of the Hebrew people when Yahweh obliterated the gods of Pharaoh. You notice that these people are multicultural. The people were divided up into twelve groups nearly forty years earlier. They were given tribal names outside of their Hebrew affiliation. They were named after the sons of Jacob whose name was changed to Israel. (*Mental shift*) In my opinion, multiculturalism today is a code word for segregation.

One of the men in the room with you asks, "What are you reading?" Your reply is "The New Testament scriptures from the Bible." "That's nice" comes his reply. A few moments pass and he asks, "What is the New Testament and what is the Bible?" He continues, "Have you ever read the unlimited works of the Torah based on the living son of God, and do you know who Moshe is?"

Perhaps you have yet to realize that the Passover Feast, the Feast of Unleavened Bread, the Feast of First Fruits, and the Feast of Weeks (or Pentecost) are the preamble (the planned repetition of the telling of an event yet to happen) for the death of the Messiah. The burial of the Messiah, who was without sin (Unleavened), the resurrection of the Messiah and the giving of the Holy Spirit (Ruach Hokedesh) fifty days after He was resurrected are all being fulfilled during His life.

You are Christian in your thought. None of these people knew what a Christian was. (contemplate a *Mental Shift*) All these people knew of this information. They were given the task of bringing it forward to all the nations and this is exactly what they did, especially the tribe of Judah. (More concerning Judah later.) Every time the Bible is opened, this is proven true.

II Timothy 3:16
"All scripture is given by inspiration of God, and is profitable for doctrine, for reproof, for correction, for instruction in righteousness."

71

Paul was writing the New Testament, but was speaking about the Old Testament scriptures. The New Testament scriptures were not a historical study at that time; they were being written as current events!

Imagine being transported to the time of Jesus (Yeshua). There is a musty room full of angry, bitter men (most of whom are priests), possibly inside the Hall of Hewn Stones within the second Temple. It is approximately 1,500 years later. The Torah is now a bunch of confusion. Everyone is arguing over the Law of Moses. Moses had no laws.

Imagine being in the court of the Sanhedrin. It was before this court the apostles Peter, John, and Paul, as well as Stephen, had to defend themselves. Our Messiah stood before this court, too. (Matt. 26:59, Mark 14:55, 15:1, Luke 22:66, John 11:47, Acts 4:15, 5:21, 6:15, 22:30, 23:1). You are witnessing the Messiah, the living Torah, proclaim that He is the Law, the instructions given to Moses, the son of God who now is being inspected (so too, were the lambs of Passover). He is being questioned by the full Sanhedrin, before being handed over to Pontius Pilate. Now imagine sitting in the audience chamber listening to the proceedings. Matthew and Peter are seated next to you.

During a lull in the activity, you begin to thumb through your Bible, stopping at the book of Matthew. You are excited that he, the very writer, is seated next to you. Matthew leans over and whispers, "Do you believe that this man before us is the one who spoke to Moses?" You answer, "Yes I do." Matthew continues, "What are you reading, friend?" You are bursting inside and answer, "The New Testament scriptures from the Bible!" He replies, "That's nice; what is the New Testament and what is the Bible?"

Your beliefs and faith were not prepared for these men to have absolutely no clue as to what you were reading. In your biblical understanding, you are not sure what the Hall of Hewn Stone is all about or what the Sanhedrin were doing in the temple in the first place. Your mind is void of most of what occurred in the temple, and yet Jesus/Yeshua taught in the temple regularly (but not from the New Testament). Yeshua told King David exactly how he wanted the temple to be built.

I Chronicles 28:11

"All this, said David, the Lord made me understand in writing by his hand on me, even all the works of this pattern."

The reason you began to thumb through your Bible was because you needed answers. (Greek thinking requires answers, but Hebrew thought follows patterns.) Here you are, looking at a Jewish man in tattered robes standing before the court of an oppressed people in the second Temple. Often our Lord taught on the Sabbath; after all, these were his commandments to Moses. You find it odd that these men of the court are arguing over the very commandments he gave to Moses. The Lord who is without spot or blemish is being examined, just as was the Passover lamb by the priests, and they are rejecting the law (the Torah). How could they have gotten so much wrong in 1,500 years? It has become even worse; this is exactly what we are doing today...a repetition of history, a pattern!

Your alarm clock begins to blare, time to get up and face another day. As you go through your day, two thoughts swirl around in your head. In your dream, the one fellow of the Hebrew people knew that the YHVH, the son of God, gave Moses the book of instruction or Torah, yet Matthew did not know what the New Testament was, and neither knew what the Bible was. Perhaps the Holy Spirit planted these two thoughts into your brain, using a dream to do so. Over the next several days, you begin to search out the answers in God's word. You experience an epiphany that changes everything! These men were clueless about the Bible, yet they are the characters we read about every time we open the pages; their concepts, relationship to, and very experiences are the story and we are the interpreters. We look back; they looked forward.

I have called this chapter, *Mental Shift* because we really do need to shift back to the beginning of the word of YHVH. We need to become *Un-Colored* by race and religion as well as the doctrines that now exist as a result. This is where *Un-Coloring* ourselves is going to be very difficult and challenging. This book (and the reasons behind writing it) is going to ask you to consider much.

What you may or may not believe concerning the entire work found in your Bible matters very little when we stop and simply realize that our creator is unlimited and so are His words, His messages, and His abilities to

73

communicate an unlimited amount of information to us all.

If you ask the question, "Why didn't I know about the Jewishness of Jesus?" and then look in the Bible for answers, you will begin to see how unlimited the Bible is; it will blow your mind. You will find Him in virtually every story, every pattern, and every life. When my mind was blown that way, the idea for this book was born. It is time to share my story. More importantly, it is my time to shout to the world, "There is hope!" I am living what hope brings to a broken life.

If you never have read the Bible, you are being robbed and stolen from; you just don't know it! If you are a rock-solid Christian, may God bless you but may he also illuminate all that led us to the Gospels via the Hebrew people, none of whom were Christian.

If you are a Jewish person who does not acknowledge the deity of Yeshua, I am sorry for what 1,800 years of the church of Constantine has done to your people, truly sorry. I am equally sorry if you are not able to see and/or understand the Messiah's first coming, based upon the thousands of years the Jews have handed down His story to all of us through the Holy Scriptures. At the end of the day, however, I am ecstatic that you have done what you have done. Perhaps the way all of this unfolds in the end will cause me to eat a few of these words. Whatever the case, I will be your friend and supporter until my death.

If you are Muslim, Hindu, Buddhist and anything else outside Judiasm or Christianity, your gods are about to be destroyed! If you are one who simply does not believe in anything, please take this opportunity to carefully consider the material presented in this book.

Exodus 33:11

"And the LORD spoke to Moses face to face, as a man speaks to his friend. And he turned again into the camp: but his servant Joshua, the son of Nun, a young man, departed not out of the tabernacle."

Moses and Yeshua were friends of an extraordinary measure. You have to mentally picture the Lion of the tribe of Judah's friendship with Moses, his servant. Their relationship was unique. The Lord even reiterated his fondness for Moses in the following reference:

74

John 5:46

"Had you believed Moses, you would have believed Me; for he wrote of Me."

Moses wrote the Torah (the first five books -- Genesis, Exodus, Leviticus, Numbers, and Deuteronomy). Many of us now realize these books are all about Jesus (Yeshua). Certainly they are about the God of Abraham.

We also realize our Messiah spoke to Moses face-to-face, as well as writing upon the tablets of stone. He wrote about Himself, and gave it to a fellow Hebrew. And guess what? None of those Hebrews were Christian!

The most amazing thing about what I just wrote is that when you reconnect Yeshua (Jesus) to the story of His Torah and what He was doing with Moses, many of the hidden truths found in the word of the Lord are not hidden at all.

This chapter has focused on shifting concepts back to the Hebrew identity of the writers of the entire word of the Lord, and Torah. It is about unlearning 1,800 years of a concept that lacks the very things that the Lord commanded Moses to teach the children of Israel, who were commanded to teach it to all of us. Every time you open your Bible, it is there. However, many of us see the entire story from a perspective that was born only 1,800 years ago, not 3,500 years ago.

Those Hebraic people learned how to see the Lord through circular thought processes and repetition via His voice, His charge, His commandments, His statutes, and His Laws. Abraham understood this about the Lord as well.

Genesis 26:4-5

"4And I will make your descendants multiply as the stars of heaven; I will give to your descendants all these lands; and in your seed all the nations of the earth shall be blessed; 5because Abraham obeyed My voice and kept My charge, My commandments, My statutes, and My laws."

In the dream mentioned earlier, Yeshua did not look like Oral Roberts (US Christian Evangelist) or the Pope of the Catholic Church. His temple robes were torn and his appearance was that of one who was incarcerated.

Prior to his arrest, and on more than one occasion, he would have looked very similar to the picture of a priest on the following diagram.

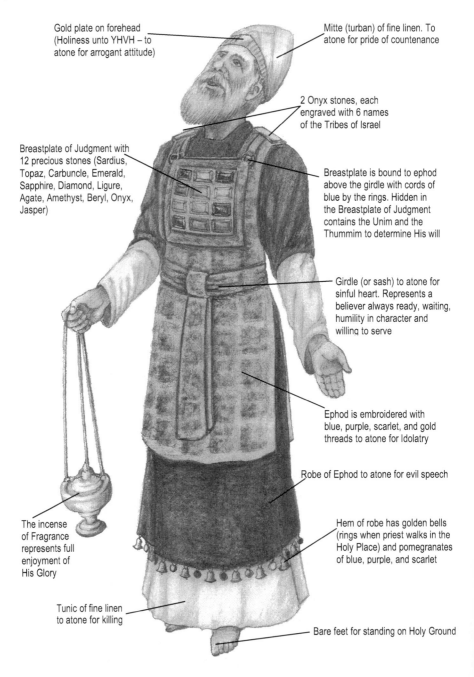

Gold plate on forehead (Holiness unto YHVH – to atone for arrogant attitude)

Mitte (turban) of fine linen. To atone for pride of countenance

2 Onyx stones, each engraved with 6 names of the Tribes of Israel

Breastplate of Judgment with 12 precious stones (Sardius, Topaz, Carbuncle, Emerald, Sapphire, Diamond, Ligure, Agate, Amethyst, Beryl, Onyx, Jasper)

Breastplate is bound to ephod above the girdle with cords of blue by the rings. Hidden in the Breastplate of Judgment contains the Unim and the Thummim to determine His will

Girdle (or sash) to atone for sinful heart. Represents a believer always ready, waiting, humility in character and willing to serve

Ephod is embroidered with blue, purple, scarlet, and gold threads to atone for Idolatry

Robe of Ephod to atone for evil speech

The incense of Fragrance represents full enjoyment of His Glory

Hem of robe has golden bells (rings when priest walks in the Holy Place) and pomegranates of blue, purple, and scarlet

Tunic of fine linen to atone for killing

Bare feet for standing on Holy Ground

The Lord did not recognize Caiphas as the High Priest, but rather John the Baptist. Our Lord's ministry did not begin until after John the Baptist died. There can be only one High Priest. The Lord assumed His natural role as the heavenly High Priest of the Order of Melchizedek after the death of John. I recommend you look into the order of the Heavenly Temple from a Hebraic construct. (I will not deprive you of that study in this book.)

(*Mental Shift*) Our Lord was Jewish. He has been walking us through His plan since the Garden of Eden. The most amazing thing you will discover in the lives of these people, the words they spoke, the alphabet they used, the letters they wrote, the mistakes they made, and the truth imprinted into them, is repeated over and over and over again century after century. He is unveiling who He is through the Jewish people of the Tribe of Judah. Judah was the fourth-born son of Jacob; his mother was Leah. All these people were Hebrews. Jacob had 12 sons nearly 500 years before Moses. The women who gave birth to all of these sons numbered four. Jacob, whose name later was changed to Israel, had one daughter as well. Her name was Dinah. If you don't know the story of Jacob's life and the children born to him, and if you don't understand the Hebrew culture of the day, you won't have a proper concept about Jacob's son, Judah, who initiated approximately 2,500 years of lineage leading up to the birth of our Messiah. You will have to force a *mental shift* in your thinking in order to follow the amazing hidden facts placed into this family and the culture which was created for them via the Lord on Mount Sinai. This chapter will challenge you, but first you have to completely *Un-Color yourself* of just about everything.

If you answered the question about knowing the Jewishness of Jesus by saying, "Not Much" earlier in this book, it is at this point I pray you will return to the beginning of the story and relearn it, or unlearn the very things that caused you to say, "Not Much."

Our lord was Jewish; we have established this and canreadily agree, but the question remains why we don't know very much about

His Jewishness. This is a key component of why we must revisit the Holy Scriptures and mentally shift back to the original mindset of these people verses the mindset of Christianity, and particularly that of Western Christianity which has developed over the course of the last 1,800 years.

If you will allow me to offer a way to help accomplish that mental shift, I would like to explain *linear thinking* versus *Hebraic thinking* as a premise for us to operate in, and a starting point in Chapter Seven: Jesus was Jewish.

Chapter Six:
Before Kunta Kinte

ॐ•७ ॐ•७ ॐ•७

Proverbs 7:2

Keep my commandments, and live; and my law as the apple of your eye.

৩৯•৫ ৩৯•৫ ৩৯•৫

I thought the following article written by a personal friend, Mr. Victor Sharpe, would address the heart of this chapter. (*Thank you, Mr. Sharpe*). Reprinted here with full permission.

Embracing Islam
(By Victor Sharpe) Extract:

Why would African-Americans who understandably abandon their current WASP (White Anglo Saxon Protestant) slave names, then choose to adopt Muslim names when Muslim Arabs enslaved black Africans for centuries? The Arab slave trade in Black Africa lasted from the late seventh century to 1911. Some estimate that the number of male and female Africans who were cruelly enslaved by the Arab Muslim traders could be as high as 14 million. How many young black Americans, willingly converting to Islam, know anything about how the Arab slavers embittered the lives of their ancestors?

The beltway sniper, John Mohammed, a black convert to Islam, was driven to shoot people at random and terrorize a large area of the East Coast. Mark Fidel Coul, another black convert to Islam, became Ansar Akba, and went as a soldier to Kuwait where he threw three grenades into his officer's tent and then shot down wounded soldiers as they ran out in distress and confusion. He murdered two soldiers and left several others badly hurt. His crime was committed because his Muslim faith became more important to him during the war in Iraq than his American citizenship.

But why do so many African-Americans embrace Islam? Perhaps the question should be why do they choose to abandon their White Anglo Saxon Protestant (WASP) names, which their ancestors were given in slavery, and replace them with Arabic names? Make no mistake — the Muslim Arabs enslaved black Africans for centuries and with devastating effect. The Arab slave trade began soon *after* the Arabs embraced the new faith of Mohammed – Islam.

In the eighth century, hordes of Arab tribesmen poured into North and East Africa offering the Africans the stark choice of the sword or forced conversion. At first, the Arabs mingled with the black Africans, but as Islamic prosperity grew, they began to denigrate the blacks. One Arab poet wrote "God put no light in the complexion of the children of a stinking Nubian (black)." Even in the early days of Islam, the Arabs' own writings displayed anti-black sentiments.

The Arab Slave Trade was a centuries-long era of torment and horror for the African blacks. Cries of terror echoed throughout countless African villages upon news of the approaching Arab slavers. But the Arabs eventually enlisted terrified Africans into becoming slavers in their own right.

80

These African converts rationalized that if they became Muslims then their position would be elevated above their fellow Africans. The real reason, however, for these Africans to embrace Islam and become slavers of their own people was simple fear for their own safety and survival. Often the Arabs would play African tribes against each other, allowing the tribal wars to weaken the resolve of the Africans and then enslave the best and strongest from among the survivors. One wonders how many young black Americans know this history of Africa and of how the Arab slavers embittered the lives of their ancestors? How many of these willing black converts to Islam know how the Arab Muslim slavers operated?

Do they know, or even care, that the Arabs would raid their villages at night killing all Africans who resisted or who tried to run away? Do they know that most of the adult men were killed off, as the Arabs preferred black women and children to be their slaves? Do they know that their ancestors endured tortuous marches through the African landscape, bound by hand and neck, as their Arab masters sought yet more African slaves? In addition, do they know, or care, how many Africans endured beatings and rapes, while others died from Arab cruelty and were dragged along by the living, still roped together in processions of the damned?

If these African slaves survived the marches and the long journeys in the black airless and stinking holds of slave ships, they were then further de-humanized in the Arab slave markets where Muslim men would inspect the human cargoes. Black women and young girls were probed in a demeaning fashion by Arab men to determine the sexual worth of their human purchases. Throughout East Africa, these scenes were repeated for centuries and slaves who were not purchased became food for the hyenas, which gorged themselves on multitudes of dead blacks.

The sexual abuse of black Africans, primarily women and girls, went on for 1,200 years and was accompanied by equally

81

horrific enslavement by the Arabs of young African boys who were routinely castrated at the ages of 8 to 12 years to serve as eunuchs. It is estimated that hundreds of thousands of African boys were treated in such a manner with many bleeding to death from cruel castrations. The Arab slave trade in Black Africa lasted from the late seventh century to 1911. Some estimate that the number of male and female Africans who were enslaved by the Arab Muslim traders could be as high as 14 million.

When African-Americans shed their white Anglo-Saxon Protestant slave names, yet eagerly adopt Arab slave names, something is very wrong with the picture. It is by all means quite legitimate to throw off WASP sounding names and embrace African names. That would be both honorable and logical. However, to embrace both the Arab names and the Muslim faith of their erstwhile slave masters, who tormented them for dark centuries, stretches credulity. Simply put, why exchange one slave name for another?

Victor Sharpe is quite correct with much of his analysis concerning African slavery under Islamic rule. The resurgence of slavery, for example, is rearing its ugly head again in Africa. Sudan and numerous other African nations are being turned into rivers of blood as a result of sin. The current genocide of anything non-Islamic is occurring throughout the Horn of Africa. Christians and Christianity, among other faiths, are systematically obliterated by killing those who practice them, and enslaving those who survive. The Horn of Africa is reliving history yet again, while at the same time, the desires to push Israel into the Mediterranean blare out of the speakers of many taxi cabs in Dearborn, Michigan, unabated.

What is different about any period of human history where the horrors of human slavery are recorded? The answer is *"Not Much!"* Hitler represented the same propensity to kill people as did historical tyrants who no doubt were deranged, but ever present throughout human history. We are the people who continue to produce the same tools used to effect genocide. Radical Islam was radical in the 5th century, too! The British Empire[1] did not ask to colonize nearly everything for 1,200 years.

82

During the machinations of the Babylonian system of Baal, or the nations that began to rise as a result of collapse of the Ottoman Empire, great harm befell the world's Jews. In today's current climate, the United States of America is doing what Britain did earlier   concerning Israel. The price to be paid will be similar as well.

We are beginning to see the prestige of the United States crumble. This, too, is tied to Israel and the treatment of her people. The relationship to the God of creation and Israel is striking. Many former tyrants do not exist, nor do their empires. After the re-birth of the nation of Israel, her language and accomplishment has been, literally, supernatural. No nation on earth can compare to her rebirth.

Many in today's thinking blame demonic strongholds or evil supernatural forces at work for just about everything. Although I certainly don't discard evil, the Holy Scriptures share a thought or two concerning the evil that men commit as well:

Genesis 13:13

"But the men of Sodom were wicked and sinners before the LORD exceedingly." In the King James translation the word wicked is employed over 325 times.

The Bible recounts a man so wicked that God himself killed him.

Genesis 38:7

"And Er, Judah's firstborn, was wicked in the sight of the LORD; and the LORD slew him."

This is an interesting passage considering Judah also produced the lineage of the Messiah. Imagine, this child Er was so wicked the Lord took him out. I can't help but think that this child had the ability to mess up centuries of unfolding history if left to his own devices. (I will have to

---

1. Interesting note concerning England. When it tossed Israel under the bus via the Belfour Declaration backstep (in my opinion) by not insisting on honoring the promises made to Israel, the steady decline of Britain began. In 1922 the *White Paper* or the *Churchill White Paper* which appeased the Arabs was made to literally stop a Middle East war between two Arab warlords (when you read between the lines). The British Empire capitulated to the Kingdom of Saud and the Hashemite Arabs. As a result, when you understand the nature of our Heavenly King, Hitler decapitated England (so to speak) just as England decapitated the Ottoman Empire. Evil was allowed to do what evil does.

83

study this more. The more I look at why this fellow, Er, appears at all in biblical history, the more I recognize that his story is making a connection to a theme.)

I have studied much since looking back through the pages of history. I have read the works of Rudolph Windsor, in particular *From Babylon to Timbuktu* and *The Valley of Dry Bones: The Conditions That Face Black People in America.* I have read countless articles, talked to many so-called Black Hebrew Israelites, and read Alex Haley's masterful work *Roots.*

I am familiar with the history of the Khazar Empire, the Kharaite controversy, and a host of topics concerning black people and biblical history. I have read the Quran, brushed up on Buddhism, and researched ancient religions. Frank M. Snowden's *Blacks in Antiquity* is a very good archeological look back and highly recommended. My point in all of this is that we missed the obvious. Our Creator fashioned a people, and then was born into this earth through them.

Jesus (Yeshua) was Jewish; this as the cornerstone of why I am writing this book looking into why he chose to come into this world Jewish, and it has *un-colored* all of what I have read. What is being revealed in his work is beyond miraculous, if such a thing can be said.

As I peer into what Judaism teaches, I see a world that I did not know existed. It is perplexing to me that the issue over the deity of Messiah is missed. On the other hand, when you really dig into the pagan worship that follows truth through the centuries, it becomes rather obvious. It also becomes rather obvious that all of us, including Judaism, were affected.

Baal worship was just as prevalent in the desert with Moses as was the sand. (I am referencing a particular ancient religion, of course.) The story of Nimrod introduces a counterfeit to the truth that literally is found in virtually every religion on earth.

Leviticus 26:1

"You shall not make for yourselves idols, nor shall you set up for yourselves an image or a sacred pillar, nor shall you place a figured stone in your land to bow down to it; for I am the LORD your God."

Well, doing so was as much a part of Israel as it was to most people during the time of the Exodus. (A good book is recommended here, *Myths and Legends* by Neil Philip.)

For the purpose of this book and for keeping this very simple, black folk did not fall out of the sky as a result of slavery. Equally, the African people did not scurry into the bush as a result of being chased with nets for the expressed purpose of captivity. The African was sold for centuries as a business transaction. The Islamic Empire enslaved entire civilizations as it spread across the "dark" continent. The identities of several kingdoms were utterly destroyed, or judged, depending on how much you know about our Savior. Moses knew him face to face, and Joshua killed thousands due to what Yeshua commanded.

The same is true for every conquering people throughout history. All history records the activity of people, from every race on this earth. To think something other than this to be true is simply ridiculous! Nevertheless, many people have a mindset that is limited to a couple of hundred years or less. (I don't mean to infer that we are on some sort of chess board of the gods, but when was the last time the King of creation was caught off guard?) What I am saying is that we repeat our history because we don't know it. How many times do you boil gasoline on the stove? Once, if you are an old friend of mine.

The simple truth is that when one begins to dig into actual history, it becomes rather easy to deconstruct long held beliefs that really never were true in the first place. The best example of this is when I ask people what they know about the Jewishness of Jesus. Ninety-nine percent of the people have said, "Not Much." I would have said the same thing four years ago. The facts speak for themselves, but for 1,800 years our minds were not taught what this actually meant. When I ask the question, "What is meant when Jesus is referred to as the Lion of the tribe of Judah?" (Revelation 5:5) The answer across the board is, "He was a descendant of Judah." Well, who is Judah and why did the Messiah chose to come into the world through Judah's family centuries before he was actually born?" (Much the same is true about knowing anything at all about the Jews.)

This leads to more questions, but our minds are trained to not even ask them. Take a brief moment to think about that and the implication made! You have just realized the power and influence of Replacement Theology. Consider why I am writing a chapter entitled *Before Kunta Kinte*. The truth: many learned to know the story, but not the evolution of slavery. The story occurred long before America and England. Slavery is not an invention of white Europeans. The form of slavery that most people have endured is a direct result of disobedience to righteousness, which is revealed by hearing and obeying Torah.

Our God is a just God, and he punishes wickedness. Israel is the best example but not the only one. There was a time in world history when every race, including the Nubian race, committed atrocities that spanned centuries. All wickedness, all evil, and all sin is punished. Judah's first born, Er, testifies to this. Sodom and Gomorrah testify to this, and our best and most recent example is Adolph Hitler. True to world history, there is always another madman rising up for the expressed purpose of tyranny. Hitler enslaved Europe, but this is not the same thing, I suppose, to those who still worship him.

I am watching the news as I write this; a black man is yelling, "Kill all Crackers!" Imagine for a moment the world that he would create. Adolph Hitler was shot in the head and subsequently burned. I watched a very specific video where this was done to Nazi victims. "Killing all Crackers" invites a certain death that has yet to escape anyone who glorifies killing because they don't like someone. (Personally, I eat crackers with soup, sometimes with chili and I do love my Cheese Whiz on crackers.) The black man yelling this nonsense will possibly one day be that child of God that the demons are tormenting for eternity. Let us hope that this fellow's heart is restored so that his brain will once again work.

Before I digress too far... Prior to Islam was the Byzantine Empire and Constantinople. What happened to the Jews during this period of history makes what the American slave experienced pale in comparison. I encourage you to take a look at that history. (My purpose in this book is not to cover history, but to lightly touch on some key aspects of actual events.) Nevertheless, if many in America knew the horror that was perpetuated upon Africa for centuries, perhaps the need to study history prior to England and certainly America would be a noteworthy cause.

Why we over look the atrocities committed against virtually every generation that has ever existed when dealing with the American slave issue is demonic, in my opinion. I suppose the emotional damage caused many to hang onto something that God himself dismantled. How many times has emotional damage due to slavery been repeated over the last 6,000 years? The racist would do well to answer this question. The people of faith need only read the biblical scriptures.

Forgiveness for our failures is tantamount to moving forward. Simply put, it is counterproductive to follow anyone who clings to unforgiveness. (Trust me when it comes to the area of unforgiveness.) How many years of proof do we need? I needed thirteen, and the cost was pain and suffering for people I love and who love me. I have realized that sometimes the Father has to step in and untangle us from personal unforgiveness. It all is relevant.

Abba Father, according to His purpose, produced on this planet the birth of America and set into motion something spectacular. An event is happening that Christianity may only recognize in part. America is more than a place for the free, or a place for Christianity to flourish.

Insofar as many believers in western Christianity don't know much about the Jewishness of Jesus, that does not mean we are not part of what God is doing. America is proof. Who are the scattered of Israel? This question must, at the very least, be explored. If Israel was scattered time and time again, and if Abraham's lineage is to be as numerous as the stars, then America is not the thought of a few white folks alone. America is God ordained based upon the plans of his Son.

In this book, I direct my next statement to black lovers of the God of Abraham, Isaac and Jacob. The God of creation used America to break the back of 1,500 years of Islamic slavery. Would someone please take this truth to the unsaved, and certainly to those who voted because of race! In my opinion, the *Content of Character* idea of Dr. Martin Luther King Jr. went out the window with the election of 2008 in America.

Today, I am a Jew lover! No other country in the history of the world has been reborn. No other language on planet earth has been restored, that I know of. For years we have been taught to be born again as

87

Christians. Then out of the plan of God, His family is reborn. What part of Christianity can ignore this miracle? Dare I say that we have been practicing such an event vicariously joining Jacob's family, Israel, for nearly 1,800 years? A season is upon us that demands that we know this information and why. Equally, our Jewish brothers and sisters who taught to us virtually everything we know about Yeshua (unless the twelve disciples were actually aliens from Caprica) need our support. First, however, they need us to know what pagan worship is and who Baal really was, so we can understand why they run from our Greek Jesus.

I love the Lord, but if I were Jewish I would not accept Jesus Christ if my life depended on it! This has actually been the mind of the Jewish people for centuries. The blood of many of their descendents screams out of the earth, a direct result of Christianity and "In the Name of Jesus." Unlike any other people in world history, the Jew without fail is blamed for just about everything wrong in the world. This is true in just about every century as well. I challenge you to prove me wrong.

Even in the Exodus story, the Hebrews were attacked by Amalek.

Exodus 17:8
"Then came Amalek, and fought with Israel in Rephidim."

This has been occurring ever since, every generation. The question as to why this is so is at hand. One must know the Hebraic patterns of our Heavenly Father in order to begin to comprehend the story. Notice I did not formulate an answer or offer one. *Before Kunta Kinte* and Alex Haley's *Roots* is the story of the horror, tragedy, disobedience, and celebrations of God's chosen people, Israel.

For those who don't know much about the Jewishness of Jesus, perhaps the answer can be found when the lie is exposed. To some, this book is leading you to explore the very reason why you follow and believe in our savior but don't know anything about his Jewish identity. The fact that at the age of twelve, Yeshua was teaching in the Temple has so many implications it would cause you to lose your breath! The number twelve is a clue but also the fact that he did so at this age is an even bigger clue.

If you know next to nothing about what was done in the temple, why, where, and by whom, then you miss the very personality of God in its construct. The Temple is an image of Yeshua, just as are you and I. He is in every detail; the very life force, the cornerstone of Israel. God did not change his personality because of Christianity, but much changed about his identity as a result of Christianity.

I named this chapter *Before Kunta Kinte* because much is taken for granted. I can prove it quite easily, I might add. If I were to ask a 16 year old black child of this current generation, "Who is Kunta Kinte?" the answer will be, I can almost guarantee, "I have no idea!" Hebraic repetition is why God exists in the patterns of how he told the Israelites to do things. They still do them through the Jews; thus the scripture:

Psalms 60:7
"Gilead is mine, and Manasseh is mine; Ephraim also is the strength of my head; Judah is my law giver"

One must understand who Judah is and why this scripture is pointed out many times. The two words "Law Giver" are His, not mine.

An article by Michael A. Hoffman II, "The Forgotten Slaves," addresses the slave trade long before blacks were chained to posts at auction! He writes "Up to one-half of all the arrivals in the American colonies were white slaves and they were America's first slaves. These Whites were slaves for life, long before Blacks ever were. This slavery was even hereditary. White children born to white slaves were enslaved too."

All the history is there; one simply needs to look for it. The truth is, of course, predicated on one looking for it; much is skewed. Thank God for the Holy Scriptures, the greatest barometer of truth that we have. Nevertheless, caution must be exercised in how you study this magnificent revelation. The Bible is a masterpiece, a literary work that is supernatural in its construction. It is purposed for all of us, and factually delivered to all of us, through the Hebrews. Every time you open your Bible, you prove what they were willing to do and what they did not do so well. Many of us read about their lives and then judge them.

God created the Hebrew people; they did not create him. In the desert and after Pharaoh, multiculturalism was born. Joshua led this people, who

89

were given a supreme set of instructions, into a land where everyone wanted to kill them and also kill their freedom. This very statement begs the question: Who knew anything at all about what God was doing with the Israelites prior to the Exodus? Forty years later, most everyone wanted to kill them as opposed to make peace. This is true nearing 4,000 years later as well. The Hebrews (and the mixed multitude of Egyptians) traveled around the desert producing an entire generation of Europeans-- right? The truth is that this celebrated history of the Exodus out of Egypt perpetuated the continuing development of the 70 nations born out of the flood.

Anti-Semitism exists in the biblical translations. For centuries, someone is always attempting to wipe the Jews out of existence. This was how paganism twisted the original scripture in order to wipe Jewish thought out of the text. Racism is the stepchild of anti-Semitism; however, the history of racism is an evolution of one nation conquering another. Greece conquered the known world, giving birth to the Roman Empire. The dark continent Africa, the so called cradle of civilization, has been through hell as a result. The African continent became the battleground for competing religions, as well as racial division. Anti-Semitism is the product of one nation rejecting the God of Abraham, Isaac and Jacob. (We don't call Hinduism anti-semitic against Islam, do we? The same theme is true with racism. The English are not racially against the Scotts.)

It was socially acceptable for black folks, globally, to be thought of as something less than, or not quite capable. A sort of mindset has been prevalent in this thinking for nearly 3,000 years. This fact is not because of the attitudes of Southern white men who lived 150 years ago. Historically, this has been true. If you understand this much and hate the Jews (who have been through 3,500 years of hell or worse) while sitting in your church thumbing through the holy scriptures that is covered in their blood....you are totally and completely blind. Your salvation is man-made and hate inspired.

In the movie *Cleopatra*,[1] all of the servants were black folk. Director Cecil B. DeMille himself was a Sephardic Jew. This is reason enough to

---

1. *Cleopatra* was released in 1934 by Paramount Pictures, directed by Cecil B. DeMille,

hate the Jews, according to one individual who pointed this out to me! Cecil B. DeMille made a movie, he did not blindfold young Iraqi boys and walk them off four story buildings.

The funny escapades of the Three Stooges, Moe, Larry and Curly, often involved a hapless black man who was always the first to run away. Well, is that reason enough to hate the Jewishness of the Stooges, while laughing at the comedy? The attempts made to wipe the Jewish people out of existence for thousands of years, and the success of enslaving the black race, is not done because of inequality but rather hatred and sin; stupidity plays a role as well. It is just as stupid to overlook the fact that many black people were in the movies because of the Jews. Dr. Martin Luther King Junior understood this. Many of those white folks walking through Alabama with him were Jews. Black folks and Jewish folks in Hollywood are better than chains and gas chambers. What is ironic to me is that racism was alive and well, and so were blacks and Jews.

Race and skin color, or religion, are used to make a distinction, or define those conquered. Hatred and sin follows all of us through the history books. We did this to ourselves. We perpetrated this and justified it by race, religion, and sheer brutality. The Kunta Kinte of today's world is a gang-banger killing his brothers, or watching the Three Stooges while smoking dope at the home of one of God's daughters after doing a rap concert. We spend millions of dollars supporting that kind of life style! When you go into any neighborhood on earth, you will find stories of someone who was killed by someone else. When you go into the ghettos of America today... well, it was safer to do so in the sixties.

Have you ever heard of Zoroastrianism or the Mithra? If you are not familiar with this ancient religion, it may shock many of you to know how much the practice resembles Christianity as well as Catholicism. Equally, you may be surprised to find that much of what we know about New Testament theology is a direct result of the paganism of this ancient Persian religion, Zoroastrianism. For some reason, many who follow Christianity do not check its beliefs against what existed before the birth of the Messiah. However, if paganism crept into the teachings of Rabbi Paul (a very Jewish theologian) 1,800 years ago, what form did it take and from what religious practice did it come?

If Rabbi Paul was truly a Pharisee (Keeper of the Law), did his conversion turn him into something better than a Jewish Rabbi? Did he think following Yeshua was better than his Jewishness? Question, questions, so many questions abound when you take a little step back. Make no mistake about it, I believe in all of what is conveyed in the Brit Hadasha (New Testament). However, I am reconnecting it to the Jewishness of the writers, and not the color of any particular people.

Before Kunta Kinte could quite easily read *Before Christianity*. Black folk got off the boat 300 years ago singing about Moses and Joshua. The old Negro spirituals weren't penned because of slavery, but rather history.

Zoroastrianism mirrors much of Christianity. How do I know this? I have opened several books and looked back through the pages of history, something that would be easy for anyone to do. I found this particular chapter in a book entitled *The Mysteries of Mithra:*[2]

"Mithra was born on December 25th as an offspring of the Sun. Next to the gods Ormuzd and Ahrimanes, Mithra held the highest rank among the gods of ancient Persia. He was represented as a beautiful youth and a Mediator. Reverend J. W. Lake states: "Mithra is spiritual light contending with spiritual darkness, and through his labors the kingdom of darkness shall be lit with heaven's own light; the Eternal will receive all things back into his favor, the world will be redeemed to God. The impure are to be purified, and the evil made good, through the mediation of Mithra, the reconciler of Ormuzd and Ahriman. Mithra is the Good, his name is Love. In relation to the Eternal he is the source of grace; in relation to man he is the life-giver and mediator."

This particular religion comes with a woman who gives birth to a king, and so on and so on. The entire study took me to the ancient Baal worship of Nimrod and Semiramis of the Tower of Babel story found in the book of Genesis. They, too, had a son whose name was Tammuz. The best DVD teaching I have found to date is *Truth or Tradition* by Jim Staley. I highly recommend you see this presentation.[3]

---

2. More information about the book by Frank Cumont entitled *The Mysteries of Mirtha*, can be found on this website: http://www.near-death.com/experiences/origen048.html
3. Consider visiting this website: www.passionfortruth.com for information on *Truth or Tradition*.

I am not writing this chapter to explain all the various studies I have completed, but rather to open a door for you, the reader, to access; and why wouldn't you? We are nearing the end of 6,000 years of failure. We have found a way to define who we are by race even in our respective faiths, only to elevate one above the other. We color ourselves away from truth. The truth for the believer remains: We are made in His image. When the Messiah comes, I am confident he will not say "All the black folks line up behind Kunta Kinte" nor "All the white people line up behind George Washington."

We are commanded to love one another, and to love our creator. I fully endorse this concept shared with us all through the chosen people of the God of Abraham, Isaac, and Jacob. I will continue to line up behind that commandment and support those people. They are the very people who populated the nations, which produced the color of us all. Un-Color yourself so you can see these people for who they really are!

Religion taught us to chuck those commandments and wipe the very people our Messiah was born from, and came to, off the face of the earth! We wiped a great deal of the Hebrew mind spoken to Moses completely out of the text as well. If you don't believe it, turn with me to the Council of Nicaea, under the leadership of Emperor Constantine.

Emperor Constantine appreciated the teachings of Zoroastrianism (with a Greek spin). He himself may not have known this, but the comparisons of what was produced at Nicaea follow the pagan beliefs of the ancient Persians like a carbon copy.

Constantine abolished the Holy Festivals that actually are the Lord's, forbad the Sabbath like so many before him, and changed everything from a Jewish revelation to us all into a church revelation for some of us.

When our Lord told Aaron and Moses to record their calendar in the book of Exodus the 12th chapter, he mapped out his Holy days as well, and made the commandments something for all the people to do (not just the Hebrews who left Egypt, but also the non-Hebrews who left with them) which includes the *believers* of today.

However, Constantine said to the whole world, "I like the Julian

93

calendar better!" His actions wiped Jewish traditions out of Christianity. Seventeen hundred years later most people are clueless about the reasons for the Hebrew calendar and the observance of the "Feasts" (or "Festivals" as some call them) of the Lord.

Some may be unfamiliar with these biblical festivals. Many people are familiar with the major holidays currently celebrated in our culture, particularly Easter, Christmas, and Thanksgiving. I encourage others to consider the holidays (Feasts) as originally established by our Creator, who commanded Israel to observe and celebrate, and rightly so. This is clearly reflected in the scriptures of the Bible that is being carried to church by so many people on Sunday. Jesus observed all of these festivals including Purim and Hanukkah. Easter, Thanksgiving, and Christmas were not holidays that the King of the Jews or the Lion of the tribe of Judah would have been teaching, as was the case with all of Israel at the time. Incidentally, these Holidays are actually appointments, scheduled by God to accomplish miraculous events on these days.

The Lord was Jewish, so why wouldn't these things be presented to all of us? The Jewish believers of the first century church recognized Yeshua as the promised Messiah. The book of Acts and the epistle of John clearly tell us "that many believed." Actually, the first church appeared in the desert with Moses. Fifteen hundred years later this "church" was continued by Yeshua's Jewish disciples.

After Constantine and the name change to Jesus, many Jews said "We know who Yeshua was but we are clueless as to who Jesus is." Nearly 1,900 years later, these people still are trying to survive the absolute historical hatred that chases them through the history of a fallen world. Yet the Bible declares:

Psalm 108:8

"Gilead is mine, and Manasseh is mine; Ephraim also is the strength of my head; Judah is my lawgiver"

Before Kunta Kinte, a fellow named Jacob had twelve sons and one daughter. All of these children reveal a story that has been wiped out of theological debates for much of Christianity. Long before that, however, a very Hebrew God poured His identity into a very Hebrew people.

Long before the Exodus event, there lived a man named Isaac whose wife Rebekah gave birth to a son who was named Jacob. He produced the continuation of a story still unfolding. There is something very special about the fourth born son of Jacob, whose name is Judah. "The Lion of the tribe of Judah" was in the beginning, and he is leading us back to Him... back to the beginning.

The definition of sin means to *miss the mark*. What sin has done to all of us is add to the truth, in order for us to have reasons to deny it. Every human being alive has done so. One of the most reinforced tools we have in our arsenal is race. For centuries, the Jewish people have been scattered to various parts of the world; they and their children have been hated and murdered. We too have killed each other for centuries because of the color of our skin.

Seventy nations rose up out of the flood and seventy nations missed the mark. What color are they and who are they? (Keep in mind that Moses married a black woman of Ethiopian descent, a Midianite named Zapporah.) Why do we know more about black slavery as an evil institution, but lack the understanding to see it was not an original idea purposed for black folk alone? Why, too, are we misaligned to an identity based upon sin, as opposed to creation, within the black community? Furthermore, why all of the hate?

I began to see the natural order of life when I accepted the identity of the lives of those Jewish people recorded in the Bible. They represent all of us. The Kids of the Kingdom, unbroken, uncolored, set free! They represent the chosen people who are part of the process leading all of us to our Messiah.

Long before Kunta Kinte, other players fought for and celebrated, in anticipation, the restoration of all things. Not much has changed.

Just for the record, if you ask a Jewish person "Why did the Jews have such trouble obeying the commandments of God?" a wise Jew might answer, "We kept getting caught up in doing what the rest of humanity was doing; we colored our sin, too!" He or she would be right; he or she also would be right to add, "We passed it down through our generations, right along with the Torah." All fall short!

When the African slaves arrived in Europe and the Americas, they arrived decimated under the sword of Islam. The identity of this people was already lost via Islam, Rome and Greece. Christianity gave the gospel message to many of these people, minus the covenant made with Israel and with Judah found

Jeremiah 31:31-40:

"[31]Behold, the days are coming, says the Lord, when I will make a new covenant with the house of Israel and with the house of Judah— [32]Not according to the covenant that I made with their fathers in the day that I took them by the hand to lead them out of the land of Egypt, My covenant which they broke, though I was a husband to them,[a] says the Lord. [33]But this is the covenant that I will make with the house of Israel after those days, says the Lord: I will put My law in their minds, and write it on their hearts; and I will be their God, and they shall be My people. [34]No more shall every man teach his neighbor, and every man his brother, saying, 'Know the Lord,' for they all shall know Me, from the least of them to the greatest of them, says the Lord. For I will forgive their iniquity, and their sin I will remember no more. [35]Thus says the Lord, who gives the sun for a light by day, the ordinances of the moon and the stars for a light by night, who disturbs the sea, and its waves roar (The Lord of hosts is His name): [36]If those ordinances depart from before Me, says the Lord, then the seed of Israel shall also cease from being a nation before Me forever. [37]Thus says the Lord: If heaven above can be measured, And the foundations of the earth searched out beneath, I will also cast off all the seed of Israel for all that they have done, says the Lord. [38]Behold, the days are coming, says the Lord, that the city shall be built for the Lord from the Tower of Hananel to the Corner Gate. [39]The surveyor's line shall again extend straight forward over the hill; then it shall turn toward Goath. [40]And the whole valley of the dead bodies and of the ashes, and all the fields as far as the Brook Kidron, to the corner of the Horse Gate toward the east, shall be holy to the Lord. It shall not be plucked up or thrown down anymore forever."

(The quintessential meaning of the text lacks the words "New Church" on every level; nor is the color of these people specifically addressed.)

Genesis 26:4

And I will make your seed to multiply as the stars of heaven, and will give to your seed all these countries; and in your seed shall all the nations of the earth be blessed.

This chapter in my book hopefully causes you to realize our identity is not in race but in our creator. He shared his identity to all of us through the history of the Hebrew people who then taught every Pastor, every Minister, and every Preacher on this planet how to follow a Jewish teacher. Whether it was Moses or Yeshua, it is Hebraic. Our God imprinted an unlimited amount of information in these Hebrew people via His Hebrew alphabet, Hebrew nature, and the very existence of Israel.

In summation: Long before Kunta Kinte, there were twelve Jewish men who witnessed a miracle. Prior to these men, the story was continued with several other characters. All of them are descendants of dirt! (None of these people are named P-Diddy.)

The entire story began to unfold when dirt was given an identity, molded into the image of God himself. He draped everything after the fact in royal beauty. He soon is to return to undo what sin (and not race) has done to his creation, and he is coming to Israel.

Many, many nations are surrounding Israel and calling for her destruction. Is it any wonder (or is it rather obvious) why the restoration of Israel is trying to be stopped at all cost? Christians tell us that you have to be *born again*. This is exactly what the Lord has in mind concerning Israel

I pray that the nation of Israel and all of those grafted into the commonwealth of Israel return to the Torah and accept the Besorah of the entire word of Elohim.

Chapter Seven:
Jesus was Jewish

Leviticus 26:3-4

If you walk in My statutes, and keep My commandments, and do them; Then I will give you rain in due season, and the land shall yield her increase, and the trees of the field shall yield their fruit.

My intent in writing, Jesus was Jewish is a simple one: to show that He and His earthly family of the time followed Torah. I encourage you to look up these scriptures and challenge what you know.

The following scriptures will help you to see clearly and for some of you, for the first time that He is the Torah and lived it perfectly. He did not do away with Himself. This is a misunderstanding that has followed much of Christianity for 1900 years. Prior to reading this chapter please look up these scriptures. They will help you to see the Jewishness of our Savior. He was never a Christian and neither were His followers based on our modern understanding. They were all Jews who obeyed the Torah.

Luke 2:21-24 — Jesus (Yeshua) was circumcised.

Luke 2:39-43 — His Family was Torah observant.

Leviticus explains why they were obeying these commandments nearly 1500 years later in Leviticus 23: 5, 6.

Luke 2:46-47 — Jesus (Yeshua) taught in the Temple:

Jesus (Yeshua) spoke with the Rabbis about Torah, He never quoted the New Testament.

Luke 2:51 — Jesus (Yeshua) honored his mother and Father

Exodus 20:12 — His relatives obeyed the TORAH

Luke 1:5,6 — Jesus (Yeshua) practiced what He preached

Mark 6:18-20	Matthew 5:17-19
Luke 4:14-16	Luke 4:31

Jesus (Yeshua) always kept the Sabbath. They argued over how He kept it not whether He did. He restored the words of His father, right?

John 7:22,23	John 9:14-16
Luke 6:1-9	Mark 1:21
Mark 1:29-31	Mark 1:32-34
Luke 13:10-12	Luke 14:1-5
John 5:9-11	Matthew 12:2-7
Mark 3:4-6	

People were following Yeshua because He was Torah observant and a teacher of the Law (Instructor). He is the word made flesh and then He did away with himself... think about this carefully. The New Testament (a real treasure trove) was not yet written when these words were spoken:

Matthew 7:12

Matthew 8:19 — No one would follow a teacher if He was not keeping Torah

Luke 24:25-27 — The New Testament had not been penned.

Luke 24:44-45 — The New Testament had not been penned.

2nd Timothy 3:115-17 — The New Testament had not been penned.

Jesus (Yeshua) wore Rabbinic clothing:

Luke 8:43-44 — She touched his Tsit Tsits or tassels hanging from his clothing

100

Numbers 15:38-39 — This was commanded dress of the Torah

Please learn the true Identity of our Lord while he was among men in the flesh He obeyed all of the Commandments, Statutes, and Laws. He did so...perfectly! He did not then die and say that none of this matters anymore or is now obsolete.

Every Christ-follower on the earth is following a Jew, and every lover of Jesus is a Jew lover, too! The difference between now and how I thought as a New Testament Christian is that I now know much more about Jewish people, Judaism, and how much they fight among their own spiritual identities. It is truly ironic so much separation exists within religious Jewish faiths. I have met some wonderful people who are Jewish and some who are not. This is true of all people, of course, and I am sure some have said as much about me. Here is my point: The number one Jew (Yeshua) is restoring all of the House of Jacob... we are that House, and Judah is supposed to be our teacher of the Torah. This is the most simple explanation of the Holy Scriptures. Let's take a look and see why this is relevant.

One Sunday about four years ago, I was sitting in church listening to a pastor toss the Jewish people from the time of Jesus under the bus. He was speaking about the people of Galatia, and how they were returning to the failed religion of Judaism. All who were present had turned to the book of Galatians in the Brit Hadasha or New Testament. I immediately thought, "Those people weren't returning to Judaism, they were worshipers of Hellenism and the gods of Greek mythology." I quietly said, "Lord, why do so many churches castigate the Jewish people?" A few seconds later I heard a voice whisper in my right ear, "Because I was one of them and they don't know much about my Jewishness."

For years I had been taught that the Jews were blind. I looked down at the passages that the pastor had us turn to in the book of Galatians and had an epiphany. It was as if the Lord unlocked a little tiny door that led me into a completely different mindset about how to experience His word. This has been the most amazing yet difficult experience to try to share with others. I began to thumb through the Bible sitting on my lap. I flipped to Genesis, then Exodus, and began to see something that never had occurred to me before. I thumbed through the books of the prophets, the gospels, and the letter writers. Our very unlimited creator created a nation of people to write His word to us. They wrote these books and presented them to all of us. They told the creation story, about Noah and the flood, the Exodus out of Egypt, and Joshua crossing the Jordan River with a bunch of youngsters heading into battle.

Moses was Hebrew; through his brilliance, he shared the story of Abraham and Isaac, then Jacob, his twelve sons and daughter, Dinah. The story of King Saul and King David also are part of the history of the nation of Israel. We also have the recorded works of the prophets, all due to the guiding influence of the incredible King of Kings and Lord of Lords walking us through the lives of the people who became the Nation of Israel.

These so called blind people have handed down the story of our Messiah for centuries. I realized they were not blind at all. We only know any of this because this nation was chosen to reveal the Son of the living God to all creation through the seed of Abraham. I sat back in my seat, changed.

The testimonies of my experiences are peppered throughout this book and indicated with frames so you can see and, hopefully, identify with whom we intrinsically are associated. All of us have personal trauma and failure. Nevertheless, we are a redeemed people. Our creator did not separate us by the colors of our skin; we did this ourselves. He did not divide up religions so we would be at war with one another; we did this ourselves. We have tools we use against one another, and we still do all of this as a redeemed people. Even now these things war against our souls. Meantime, He set the nation of Israel apart.

The Hebrew people, in particular the Jews, are *stoned* virtually every day of their existence. When the Lord whispered, "Because I was one of them," I then understood what He meant. I also understand why the Jewish people are maligned and chased through the pages of history by those who wish to stop the revelation of the Lion of the tribe of Judah. They insist on trying to find ways to wipe the Jews off of the map; thankfully, nothing has been successful.

102

Not even the Jewish people themselves have managed to kill off the people whom God calls the "apple of his eye" (Deuteronomy 32:10).

Zechariah 2:8-9
"For thus says the Lord of hosts, After glory He has sent me against the nations which plunder you, for he who touches you touches the apple of His eye. For behold, I will shake my hand on them, and they shall be a spoil to their servants, and you shall know that the Lord of hosts has sent me."

This has not changed, but Replacement Theology has attempted to change these scriptures for almost 2,000 years. Clearly, we can see that Islam is in for a hellish future and so, too, are those persons who hate the Jews.

My connection to the Jewish people is not because of the scriptures alone. Truly, I have met some of the most wonderful people who happen to be Jewish. I learn from them. I am amazed at the history that is alive in them. Sadly, most are secular and/or traditional. Surprisingly, many agree with those who want to kill all of them...it is bizarre! At the end of the day, though, all recognize their kinship.

After my mother returned from a trip to Israel, she said, "The most amazing aspect of Israel are the people." My mother also told me she was full of affection for them. Most of what we hear from the news and media sources is not about Israel.

I pray you may make a connection to the people of Israel and the Jewishness of our Savior through the pages of the Bible. He is found on virtually all of them. He imprinted both information and revelation into the Hebrew people. They are not blind, but like them, we all are learning this revelation under a veil. I am about to offer a key that unlocks a miracle that helped millions of people escape for nearly 2,000 years.

Prior to the birth of our Messiah, the same sort of lock was put in place that obscured the intentions conveyed to us through Moses. The Lord himself said the following:

John 5:46
"Had you believed Moses, you would have believed me; for he wrote of me"

Before we continue it is imperative that you *Un-Color* yourself from religion.

Many of us march out from our families with the tools that pain develops over years of growing up lost. We are redeemed, but have learned to live separate from our redemption. This conflict only produces more pain. It is its own addiction because the truth is not immediate but speculative. We chase after the knowledge of good versus evil, not realizing both produce death. When the Lord told me to find out why he was Jewish, his story began to leap off the pages of His word. This became overwhelming, and I continue to have what I now affectionately refer to as "Ah Ha" moments. I experience wonderful truths about him almost daily. The most interesting aspect of this is that these moments occur almost exclusively while reading the so-called Old Testament.

I have a few questions for you that will challenge you. Please don't fear them or toss them under the bus. Are you still ready?

Mary and Joseph, being Jewish, were blessed with raising our Savior. The Lord was born to this Jewish family who trained him up in the Torah and the customs and traditions that made these people Jewish. Christianity was not even a word at this time. According to Luke:

Luke 41:2
"Now his parents went to Jerusalem every year at the feast of the Passover."

Therefore, at the age of twelve, he went to the temple with them to participate in the Feast of Passover. The following passage tell us why:

Leviticus 23:4-8
4"These are the feasts of the Lord, holy convocations which you shall proclaim at their appointed times. 5On the fourteenth day of the first month at twilight is the Lord's Passover. 6And on the fifteenth day of the same month is the Feast of Unleavened Bread to the Lord; seven days you must eat unleavened bread. 7On the first day you shall have a holy convocation; you shall do no customary work on it. 8But you shall offer an offering made by fire to the Lord for seven days. The seventh day shall be a holy convocation; you shall do no customary work on it."

We see that Mary and Joseph honored this commandment and so did our Lord. Did any of you see the "Ah Ha" moment? The feast days are not Jewish but rather the Lord's and here He was going to celebrate His feast days with His earthly parents at the age of twelve. We learn that our Lord kept every one of his Feast days, taught in the temple from the five books of Moses, and obeyed everything that He told Moses to do, and to write, and to speak to the children of Israel.

Also in Leviticus, we see that the Lord is teaching them about the Passover, about 1,500 years before He became the Passover lamb. As you look at the feast days, you begin to see the Lord in all of them. This also is true of the seven days of creation.

Genesis 2:7
"And the LORD God formed man of the dust of the ground, and breathed into his nostrils the breath of life; and man became a living soul"

The Lord God, why not just God, why Lord God? Why too, was the Lord God the one who was now reaching into the dirt as opposed to, "In the beginning God created the heavens and the earth." Why the distinction? I will come back to this "Ah Ha" moment; it is a big one!

Nevertheless, our Lord followed all of the laws (Instructions) He had given to Moses. He even participated in Purim and Hanukah or The Feast of Dedication as evidenced in the following verses.

John 10:22-23
"[22]Now it was the Feast of Dedication in Jerusalem, and it was winter. [23]And Jesus walked in the temple, in Solomon's porch."

The Feast of Dedication is commemorative of Hanukkah. Imagine that! The Lord honored Hanukkah. The truth of the matter is that our Savior honored this feast and also Purim. The feast of Purim commemorates Queen Esther's role in saving Israel from Haman's plot to kill all the Jews.

The Lord taught in the temple. During the Feast of Tabernacles, he actually stood up during the Water Libation Ceremony and declared who He was:

105

John 7:10-22

"[10]But when His brothers had gone up, then He also went up to the feast, not openly, but as it were in secret. [11]Then the Jews sought Him at the feast, and said, 'Where is He?' [12]And there was much complaining among the people concerning Him. Some said, 'He is good;' others said 'No, on the contrary, He deceives the people.' [13]However, no one spoke openly of Him for fear of the Jews. [14]Now about the middle of the feast Jesus went up into the temple and taught. [15]And the Jews marveled, saying, 'How does this Man know letters, having never studied?' [16]Jesus[c] answered them and said, 'My doctrine is not Mine, but His who sent Me. [17]If anyone wills to do His will, he shall know concerning the doctrine, whether it is from God or whether I speak on My own authority. [18]He who speaks from himself seeks his own glory; but He who seeks the glory of the One who sent Him is true, and no unrighteousness is in Him. [19]Did not Moses give you the law, yet none of you keeps the law? Why do you seek to kill me?' [20]The people answered and said, 'You have a demon. Who is seeking to kill you?' [21]Jesus answered and said to them, 'I did one work, and you all marvel. [22]Moses therefore gave you circumcision (not that it is from Moses, but from the Father), and you circumcise a man on the Sabbath.'"

Again, we find the Lord not only honoring His festivals, but also teaching in the temple. He never quoted a syllable of the so-called New Testament, but he quoted the Prophets and Moses regularly.

Jesus was born Jewish to Jewish parents. He was raised up in the commandments that were given to Moses, honored the Festival days, and taught in the glorious second temple. He knew the written Torah given to Moses by finger, as it were, and the oral Torah spoken to Moses face to face. He was a Jewish Rabbi of extraordinary ability. He had to wear the rabbinical robes in order to teach in the temple, and to follow the strict manner of tabernacle worship prescribed in the book of Leviticus.

He was killed among the Jews, buried among the Jews, rose from the dead among the Jews, and taught His words for forty days after His resurrection. He sent the Holy Spirit to the upper room of the magnificent second temple, and they were filled with His Torah, His spirit. From all this, we can see that he meant to do a mighty thing among the Jewish people, and did so. What do you know about the Jewishness of those people? This question is actually the key. If you answer this question honestly, then your answer may be, "Not Much!"

I recently had a discussion with a person of Jewish descent who was emphatic about the patterns found in the Torah, and how God repeats his purposes throughout the generations. I, of course, agreed. We were talking about the perverted stories found in Baal worship, specifically about the birth of a child. This child, Tammuz, would become a god and restore good to the world. This pagan religion's concepts are peppered throughout most world religions. I understood his assertion. After listening for some time, I asked a question of my very wise friend. I asked if it was impossible for God himself to be born a child and what does the birth of any child represent as far as patterns are concerned? My friend paused but did not offer an answer. The conversation ended with no more discussion. If the birth of every child has been perverted, why would the birth of God be any different? God can raise himself and give birth to himself, right? How else do any of us understand these things? Who among us has a license to create life or to raise the dead?

I purposely have not relied on scriptures to present the information in this chapter. I encourage you to look into much of what I have written. This is what I have done, as well as challenging everything I had learned in church. Why shouldn't I? (All fall short of the mark.)

I refuse to argue with any Jewish person about the deity of Messiah. I would much rather listen to what they have been learning for centuries, or have coffee and talk about the kids! I think the bloodshed, anti-Semitism, racism, and overall insistence on being right is insanity! After all, how much has anything we've done as a collective body that inhabits one planet show us when it comes to not killing each other?

I am about to get into areas of what I have learned these last four years that, if you are willing, will blow your mind. The surprise I spoke of in the introduction is shaping up. Who of you can tell me all there is to know about the Paleo Hebrew alphabet? I would suggest to you that Yeshua is who Adam saw when he opened his eyes.

Six itty, bitty, little questions

1) When did Paul the Apostle (Rabbi Shaul) become a Christian?
2) With the exception of Judas, when did the remaining disciples become Christians?
3) What did Mary (Mariam) and Joseph know about following Christ?
4) When did their son stop being Jewish?
5) If all these people went to the temple, kept the feast days, obeyed the statutes, laws and commandments that were given to Moses, when did they give all of these up as a result of Jesus?
6) If the goal is to *know* the Lord who came to the world as a Jew through Jewish parents, chose twelve Jewish men to be His disciples, taught the things that Moses taught to virtually everyone He came in contact with, died on a feast day, was buried on a feast day, was raised up on a feast day, left 40 days later promising to return on a feast day to Jerusalem (Mount of Olives, to be precise) and then sent the Holy Spirit ten days later on a feast day, (Pentecost) to the twelve Jews (which included Mathias, who had replaced Judas) who were gathered in the upper room of the Temple, not the neighborhood synagogue...

What do you know about these Jews and their Jewishness including, the King of the Jews and or the Lion of the tribe of Judah? If the answer is "Not Much," then perhaps you know more about Waldo and don't realize it. If you truly don't know much about who He was in the flesh, why not? He created the Hebrew and the Jew, the nation of Israel, the Gentiles as well as the heathens, and the Gospel message. None of this was done by man. Whether you believe in Ben Joseph or Ben David, Jesus or Yeshua, the Messiah is coming to this earth to do exactly what He said. He comes to gather the lost sheep of the house of Israel, remarry this people, restore the identity of Judah, and lead those who endure into the one thousand years of Sabbath rest. The creator of us all has never broken a promise. The Spirit of Adonai is guiding every born-again Christian whose life is changed to ask and answer these questions. The Spirit of the God of creation is drawing all believers in the Torah to his Son. Both are being called to return to B'reisheet (Genesis).

Chapter Eight:
Hear and Obey

(What do you have to lose?)

ৡৄ•৶৾   ৡৄ•৶৾   ৡৄ•৶৾

Proverbs 3:1

My son, forget not my law; but let your heart keep my commandments:

ৡৄ•৶   ৡৄ•৶   ৡৄ•৶

This chapter introduces many terms that may not be familiar. Refer to the section in the back for a list of Hebrew terms used in this book.

Because Jesus was Jewish, these terms would have been very familiar to Him. Remember, He first created the Nation of Israel, and Moses had no concept of Christianity. I point this out because some may think of the people of Israel (the Jews) as being something other than Hebrew. Furthermore, if we are grafted into this people, it truly is time to unfold our hands and find out what they know -- not everything, but certainly what God ordained.

Hear and obey is not an order shouted across the cosmos by the God of creation, but two separate commandments. In Hebrew, it is called the *Shema*, which is found in the book of Deuteronomy.

109

The following is found on the Wikipedia[1] website:

Observant Jews consider the Shema to be the most important part of the prayer service in Judaism, and its twice-daily recitation as a mitzvah (religious commandment). It is traditional for Jews to say the Shema as their last words, and parents teach it to their children before they go to sleep at night. The words are "Shema yisrael adonai eloheinu adonai echad (silently) baruch shem kavod malchuto le'olam vaed." The term "Shema" is used by extension to refer to the whole part of the daily prayers that commence with Shema Yisrael and comprise Deuteronomy 6:4-9, 11:13-21, and Numbers 15:37-41. These sections of the Torah are read in the weekly Torah portions Va'etchanan, Eikev, and Shlach, respectively.

The father wants us to hear and do what He knows is the very best course of action as we weave our way through a fallen world. I often use the following analogy when explaining to people how much his concern is for us: Two kids are stranded on the edge of a cliff. The only way to go is back the way they came. They are frightened and as a result, fear has them arguing because of the predicament they now are in. The Father comes with outstretched arms and gently encourages these two kids of His household to hear and obey His every word! With great confidence and a soothing voice, he directs their paths back to him, to safety. The Shema is not a harsh command to obey or die but to return to Him. The Jews can spend a decade teaching on this one word alone.

The scriptures have taught it for 3,500 years. Many of us are completely and totally unaware of the depth of the prayers of Israel. I hope this book causes you to ask why, as opposed to relying on the misunderstanding found in what we have been taught concerning the Law and/or Torah. I think the Shema is absolutely and resoundingly beautiful. There is a YouTube[2] video showing the Hebrew text while the Shema is sung. I hope this video will remain as long as the printing of my book.

---

1 Wikipedia. web reference: http://en.wikipedia.org/wiki/Shema_Yisrael
2 Beyt Hillel © 2007. View the YoutTube video: http://www.youtube.com/watch?v=Fzvkr1RNZK8

The first criticism I get when closing the gap between the people who wrote the Bible and those who interpreted it for the church is that I am trying to put folks back under the law. The simple answer to this is *no*. The actual right answer is "If you were never Jewish, when were you ever under the law?" For the purpose of my book and the message contained therein, this book is not a dissertation concerning the law. I say this with complete confidence: the Jew and the Christian have a misunderstanding over this issue. The Jewish teachers initiated it, and the Christian theologians took it to another level entirely. Yeshua fulfilled the law. He was the goal of the law. His entire purpose was to demonstrate who He was through His instructions.

The study of the Hebraic root of our Messiah is causing many of us to go back and take another look. One cannot help but start with the kids of Abraham! If you really want to go further than this, unravel the word, "B'reisheet!" in the Paleo Hebrew! An excellent book for you to consider is *Creation's Heartbeat* by Dr. Yonathan Fass. (For those of you who have no idea what is unlocked in God's alphabet, Dr. Fass deals with the first four words in the Bible. He writes an entire book concerning them.)

You likely will have no idea until you take a peek at the words the Father wrote through people as His instruments while at the same time revealing the amazing. (It likely is not possible for you to comprehend what I am sharing unless and until you truly investigate these things for yourself.)

I have the added problem of not being a teacher of this material so I literally cannot teach you. I simply am opening a door for you to learn how to *hear and obey* the incredible truth. You must challenge what you know, and lay down the tools we so often have used against one another because of what we know, or think we know. None of us has the whole truth, although we tend to use what we do know to beat the living hell out of one another. Again, a door is all that I present. In so doing, I only ask that you *Un-Color* yourself from race and religion before you enter. Leave your tools and weapons outside! Again, and according to Isaiah, "He will teach us His ways." Both the Jews and the Christians think they have no need of this. By the time we are through fighting about it, God will have no need to restore anything!

111

The Torah Portion: Every week (and for hundreds of centuries), the Jews (Law Givers) recite the first five books of the Bible. The weekly Torah portions often deal with events currently taking place in the world. This has been true of every generation. (Again, the word of our creator is incredible!) At the conclusion of a year, based upon the biblical calendar, the process starts all over again. The books of Moses repeat, and are broken into weekly segments. This should give you a better understanding about how the Jews obeyed the commandment to *hear and obey*. You and I likely know what we know of the messages of the Bible in part because they did what was asked. The enemy of God has been trying to stop them ever since. They do this for us, too, and most of us don't know that they do it at all. There are many life experiences that relate to the Torah portions.

Jesus himself is found on virtually every page of the books of Moses. He even declares this out of His own mouth:

John 5:46

"Had you believed Moses, you would have believed Me; for he wrote of Me."

Equally, the book of Luke states:

Luke 24:27

"Then beginning with Moses and with all the prophets, He explained to them the things concerning Himself in all the Scriptures."

Bill Cloud writes in his book *Emnity Between the Seed* "It is at least possible that, on many occasions, what the Word reveals to us on the surface of the text may be there to teach us about what is beneath the surface of the text or the foundation."

In complete agreement, I realize that the Father is not limited at all, and well able to show to us a myriad of understanding if and when we learn how to understand the manner He chooses. He chose to do much of this through Israel, Jacob's bloodline. It is therefore crucial that we understand the Hebrew mindset as opposed to the surface interpretation of Greek thinking. I am not against the Greek translations; I think both serve a purpose, but the original construct of the Bible was not Greco-Roman.

Hearing and obeying is critical to everything found in the Holy

Scriptures. This is how the Father brings us back from the edge of a cliff. During the course of the last 1,800 years we were taught to replace *hearing and doing* with *grace*. Moses had grace, King David had grace, Abraham had grace, Noah had grace, Adam and Eve had amazing grace! None of these people knew the cross of Christianity but they all knew the covenants. They all did what He commanded of them after the fall. The only difference between Eden and Sinai was sin.

The Father did not change the rules, for He does not change. In fact, He uses strategies to help us, if we will let Him do so in the face of our willful, disobedient insistence on doing life on the edge of a cliff. The rules were made known to all of us through the Son. I suggest to you that when Adam opened his eyes he saw Jesus, Yeshuah, the Messiah.

John 8:28
"Then said Jesus to them, When you have lifted up the Son of man, then shall you know that I am He, and that I do nothing of myself; but as my Father has taught me, I speak these things."

John 1:18
"No man has seen God at any time, the only begotten Son, which is in the bosom of the Father, he has declared him..."

(Did you know that the Torah scroll is lifted up in virtually every service in the synagogues across the globe?)

Please keep in mind this book is not suggesting that you *Un-Color* yourself so you can become Jewish. This would be absurd. Our King and returning Messiah is returning to his people, Judah, in Jerusalem. We Gentiles need to know why this matters and it does matter. As a reminder, He declares that in so doing he will gather the scattered House of Israel, the Lost Sheep, with him.

Matthew 15:24
"But he answered and said, I am not sent but to the lost sheep of the house of Israel."

Hearing and obeying is far better than asking for forgiveness every second of your experience. How life has colored all of us demands that we

113

learn how to hear the voice of our Father and then do what he commands. He leads us to salvation as a result. Yeshua means *salvation*. What do you have to lose? If you fail to hear and obey God's commandments, you lose everything!

Keep My Commandments, My Statutes, and My Laws (KJV)

Ex 16:28 And the Lord said unto Moses, How long refuse ye to keep my commandments and my laws?

Ex 20:6 And showing mercy unto thousands of them that love me, and keep my commandments.

Lev 22:31 Therefore shall ye keep my commandments, and do them: I am the Lord.

Le 26:3 If ye walk in my statutes, and keep my commandments, and do them.

De 5:10 And showing mercy unto thousands of them that love me and keep my commandments.

De 5:29 O that there were such an heart in them, that they would fear me, and keep all my commandments always, that it might be well with them, and with their children for ever!

1 Kings 3:14 And if thou wilt walk in my ways, to keep my statutes and my commandments, as thy father David did walk, then I will lengthen thy days.

1 Kings 6:12 Concerning this house which thou art building, if thou wilt walk in my statutes, and execute my judgments, and keep all my commandments to walk in them; then will I perform my word with thee, which I spake unto David thy father:

1 Ki 9:6 But if ye shall at all turn from following me, ye or your children, and will not keep my commandments and my statutes which I have set before you, but go and serve other gods, and worship them:

114

1 Ki 11:38 And it shall be, if thou wilt hearken unto all that I command thee, and wilt walk in my ways, and do that is right in my sight, to keep my statutes and my commandments, as David my servant did, that I will be with thee, and build thee a sure house, as I built for David, and will give Israel unto thee.

2 Ki 17:13 Yet the Lord testified against Israel, and against Judah, by all the prophets, and by all the seers, saying, Turn ye from your evil ways, and keep my commandments and my statutes, according to all the law which I commanded your fathers, and which I sent to you by my servants the prophets.

1 Ch 29:19 And give unto Solomon my son a perfect heart, to keep thy commandments, thy testimonies, and thy statutes, and to do all these things, and to build the palace, for the which I have made provision.

Ne 1:9 But if ye turn unto me, and keep my commandments, and do them; though there were of you cast out unto the uttermost part of the heaven, yet will I gather them from thence, and will bring them unto the place that I have chosen to set my name there.

Ps 89:31 If they break my statutes, and keep not my commandments;

Ps 119:115 Depart from me, ye evildoers: for I will keep the commandments of my God.

Pr 3:1 My son, forget not my law; but let thine heart keep my commandments:

Pr 4:4 He taught me also, and said unto me, Let thine heart retain my words: keep my commandments, and live.

Pr 7:1 My son, keep my words, and lay up my commandments with thee.

Pr 7:2 Keep my commandments, and live; and my law as the apple of thine eye.

Da 9:4 And I prayed unto the Lord my God, and made my confession, and said, O Lord, the great and dreadful God, keeping the covenant and mercy to them that love him, and to them that keep his commandments;

John 14:15 If ye love me, keep my commandments.

John 15:10 If ye keep my commandments, ye shall abide in my love; even as I have kept my Father's commandments, and abide in his love.

Ge 26:5 Because that Abraham obeyed my voice, and kept my charge, my commandments, my statutes, and my laws.

Ex 15:26 And said, If thou wilt diligently hearken to the voice of the Lord thy God, and wilt do that which is right in his sight, and wilt give ear to his commandments, and keep all his statutes, I will put none of these diseases upon thee, which I have brought upon the Egyptians: for I am the Lord that healeth thee.

Ex 18:16 When they have a matter, they come unto me; and I judge between one and another, and I do make them know the statutes of God, and his laws. (one: Heb. a man and his fellow.)

Le 10:11 And that ye may teach the children of Israel all the statutes which the Lord hath spoken unto them by the hand of Moses.

Le 18:5 Ye shall therefore keep my statutes, and my judgments: which if a man do, he shall live in them: I am the Lord.

Le 18:26 Ye shall therefore keep my statutes and my judgments, and shall not commit any of these abominations; neither any of your own nation, nor any stranger that sojourneth among you:

Le 19:19 Ye shall keep my statutes. Thou shalt not let thy

cattle gender with a diverse kind: thou shalt not sow thy field with mingled seed: neither shall a garment mingled of linen and woollen come upon thee.

Le 19:37 Therefore shall ye observe all my statutes, and all my judgments, and do them: I am the Lord.

Le 20:8 And ye shall keep my statutes, and do them: I am the Lord which sanctifies you.

Le 20:22 Ye shall therefore keep all my statutes, and all my judgments, and do them: that the land, whither I bring you to dwell therein, spew you not out.

Le 25:18 Wherefore ye shall do my statutes, and keep my judgments, and do them; and ye shall dwell in the land in safety.

Le 26:15 And if ye shall despise my statutes, or if your soul abhor my judgments, so that ye will not do all my commandments, but that ye break my covenant:

Le 26:43 The land also shall be left of them, and shall enjoy her sabbaths, while she lieth desolate without them: and they shall accept of the punishment of their iniquity: because, even because they despised my judgments, and because their soul abhorred my statutes.

Le 26:46 These are the statutes and judgments and laws, which the Lord made between him and the children of Israel in mount Sinai by the hand of Moses.

Nu 30:16 These are the statutes, which the Lord commanded Moses, between a man and his wife, between the father and his daughter, being yet in her youth in her father's house.

De 4:1 Now therefore hearken, O Israel, unto the statutes and unto the judgments, which I teach you, for to do them, that ye may live, and go in and possess the land which the Lord God of your fathers giveth you.

De 4:5 Behold, I have taught you statutes and judgments, even as the Lord my God commanded me, that ye should do so in the land whither ye go to possess it.

De 4:6 Keep therefore and do them; for this is your wisdom and your understanding in the sight of the nations, which shall hear all these statutes, and say, Surely this great nation is a wise and understanding people.

De 4:8 And what nation is there so great, that hath statutes and judgments so righteous as all this law, which I set before you this day?

De 4:14 And the Lord commanded me at that time to teach you statutes and judgments, that ye might do them in the land whither ye go over to possess it.

De 4:40 Thou shalt keep therefore his statutes, and his commandments, which I command thee this day, that it may go well with thee, and with thy children after thee, and that thou mayest prolong thy days upon the earth, which the Lord thy God giveth thee, forever.

De 4:45 These are the testimonies, and the statutes, and the judgments, which Moses spake unto the children of Israel, after they came forth out of Egypt,

De 5:1 And Moses called all Israel, and said unto them, Hear, O Israel, the statutes and judgments which I speak in your ears this day, that ye may learn them, and keep, and do them. (keep...: Heb. keep to do them.)

De 5:31 But as for thee, stand thou here by me, and I will speak unto thee all the commandments, and the statutes, and the judgments, which thou shalt teach them, that they may do them in the land which I give them to possess it.

De 6:1 Now these are the commandments, the statutes and the judgments, which the Lord your God commanded to teach you, that ye might do them in the land whither ye go to possess it:

De 6:2 That thou mightest fear the Lord thy God, to keep all his statutes and his commandments, which I command thee, thou, and thy son, and thy son's son, all the days of thy life, and that thy days may be prolonged.

De 6:17 Ye shall diligently keep the commandments of the Lord your God, and his testimonies, and his statutes, which he hath commanded thee.

De 6:20 And when thy son asketh thee in time to come, saying, What mean the testimonies, and the statutes, and the judgments, which the Lord our God hath commanded you?

De 6:24 And the Lord commanded us to do all these statutes, to fear the Lord our God, for our good always, that he might preserve us alive, as it is at this day.

De 7:11 Thou shalt therefore keep the commandments, and the statutes, and the judgments, which I command thee this day, to do them.

De 8:11 Beware that thou forget not the Lord thy God, in not keeping his commandments, and his judgments, and his statutes, which I command thee this day:

De 10:13 To keep the commandments of the Lord, and his statutes, which I command thee this day for thy good?

De 11:1 Therefore thou shalt love the Lord thy God, and keep his charge, and his statutes, and his judgments, and his commandments, alway.

De 11:32 And ye shall observe to do all the statutes and judgments which I set before you this day.

De 12:1 These are the statutes and judgments, which ye shall observe to do in the land, which the Lord God of thy fathers giveth thee to possess it, all the days that ye live upon the earth.

De 16:12 And thou shalt remember that thou wast a bondman in Egypt: and thou shalt observe and do these statutes.

De 17:19 And it shall be with him, and he shall read therein all the days of his life: that he may learn to fear the Lord his God, to keep all the words of this law and these statutes, to do them:

De 26:16 This day the Lord thy God hath commanded thee to do these statutes and judgments: thou shalt therefore keep and do them with all thine heart, and with all thy soul.

De 26:17 Thou hast avouched the Lord this day to be thy God, and to walk in his ways, and to keep his statutes, and his commandments, and his judgments, and to hearken unto his voice:

De 27:10 Thou shalt therefore obey the voice of the Lord thy God, and do his commandments and his statutes, which I command thee this day.

De 28:15 But it shall come to pass, if thou wilt not hearken unto the voice of the Lord thy God, to observe to do all his commandments and his statutes which I command thee this day; that all these curses shall come upon thee, and overtake thee:

De 28:45 Moreover all these curses shall come upon thee, and shall pursue thee, and overtake thee, till thou be destroyed; because thou hearkenest not unto the voice of the Lord thy God, to keep his commandments and his statutes which he commanded thee:

De 30:10 If thou shalt hearken unto the voice of the Lord thy God, to keep his commandments and his statutes which are written in this book of the law, and if thou turn unto the Lord thy God with all thine heart, and with all thy soul.

De 30:16 In that I command thee this day to love the Lord thy God, to walk in his ways, and to keep his commandments and his statutes and his judgments, that thou mayest live and multiply: and the Lord thy God shall bless thee in the land whither thou goest to possess it.

2 Sa 22:23 For all his judgments were before me: and as for his statutes, I did not depart from them.

1 Ki 2:3 And keep the charge of the Lord thy God, to walk in his ways, to keep his statutes, and his commandments, and his judgments, and his testimonies, as it is written in the law of Moses, that thou mayest prosper in all that thou doest, and whithersoever thou turnest thyself:

1 Ki 3:3 And Solomon loved the Lord, walking in the statutes of David his father: only he sacrificed and burnt incense in high places.

1 Ki 8:58 That he may incline our hearts unto him, to walk in all his ways, and to keep his commandments, and his statutes, and his judgments, which he commanded our fathers.

1 Ki 8:61 Let your heart therefore be perfect with the Lord our God, to walk in his statutes, and to keep his commandments, as at this day.

1 Ki 9:4 And if thou wilt walk before me, as David thy father walked, in integrity of heart, and in uprightness, to do according to all that I have commanded thee, and wilt keep my statutes and my judgments:

1 Ki 11:11 Wherefore the Lord said unto Solomon, Forasmuch as this is done of thee, and thou hast not kept my covenant and my statutes, which I have commanded thee, I will surely rend the kingdom from thee, and will give it to thy servant.

1 Ki 11:33 Because that they have forsaken me, and have worshipped Ashtoreth the goddess of the Zidonians, Chemosh the god of the Moabites, and Milcom the god of the children of Ammon, and have not walked in my ways, to do that which is right in mine eyes, and to keep my statutes and my judgments, as did David his father.

121

1 Ki 11:34 Howbeit I will not take the whole kingdom out of his hand: but I will make him prince all the days of his life for David my servant's sake, whom I chose, because he kept my commandments and my statutes:

2 Ki 17:8 And walked in the statutes of the heathen, whom the Lord cast out from before the children of Israel, and of the kings of Israel, which they had made.

2 Ki 17:15 And they rejected his statutes, and his covenant that he made with their fathers, and his testimonies which he testified against them; and they followed vanity, and became vain, and went after the heathen that were round about them, concerning whom the Lord had charged them, that they should not do like them.

2 Ki 17:19 Also Judah kept not the commandments of the LORD their God, but walked in the statutes of Israel which they made.

2 Ki 17:34 Unto this day they do after the former manners: they fear not the Lord, neither do they after their statutes, or after their ordinances, or after the law and commandment which the Lord commanded the children of Jacob, whom he named Israel;

2 Ki 17:37 And the statutes, and the ordinances, and the law, and the commandment, which he wrote for you, ye shall observe to do for evermore; and ye shall not fear other gods.

2 Ki 23:3 And the king stood by a pillar, and made a covenant before the Lord, to walk after the Lord, and to keep his commandments and his testimonies and his statutes with all their heart and all their soul, to perform the words of this covenant that were written in this book. And all the people stood to the covenant.

1 Ch 22:13 Then shalt thou prosper, if thou takest heed to fulfil the statutes and judgments which the Lord charged Moses with concerning Israel: be strong, and of good courage; dread

not, nor be dismayed.

2 Ch 7:17 And as for thee, if thou wilt walk before me, as David thy father walked, and do according to all that I have commanded thee, and shalt observe my statutes and my judgments;

2 Ch 7:19 But if ye turn away, and forsake my statutes and my commandments, which I have set before you, and shall go and serve other gods, and worship them;

2 Ch 19:10 And what cause so ever shall come to you of your brethren that dwell in their cities, between blood and blood, between law and commandment, statutes and judgments, ye shall even warn them that they trespass not against the Lord, and so wrath come upon you, and upon your brethren: this do, and ye shall not trespass.

2 Ch 33:8 Neither will I any more remove the foot of Israel from out of the land which I have appointed for your fathers; so that they will take heed to do all that I have commanded them, according to the whole law and the statutes and the ordinances by the hand of Moses.

2 Ch 34:31 And the king stood in his place, and made a covenant before the Lord, to walk after the Lord, and to keep his commandments, and his testimonies, and his statutes, with all his heart, and with all his soul, to perform the words of the covenant which are written in this book.

Ezr 7:10 For Ezra had prepared his heart to seek the law of the Lord, and to do it, and to teach in Israel statutes and judgments.

Ezr 7:11 Now this is the copy of the letter that the king Artaxerxes gave unto Ezra the priest, the scribe, even a scribe of the words of the commandments of the Lord, and of his statutes to Israel.

Ne 1:7 We have dealt very corruptly against thee, and have

not kept the commandments, nor the statutes, nor the judgments, which thou commandedst thy servant Moses.

Ne 9:13 Thou camest down also upon mount Sinai, and spakest with them from heaven, and gavest them right judgments, and true laws, good statutes and commandments:

Ne 9:14 And madest known unto them thy holy sabbath, and commandedst them precepts, statutes, and laws, by the hand of Moses thy servant:

Ne 10:29 They clave to their brethren, their nobles, and entered into a curse, and into an oath, to walk in God's law, which was given by Moses the servant of God, and to observe and do all the commandments of the Lord our Lord, and his judgments and his statutes;

Ps 18:22 For all his judgments were before me, and I did not put away his statutes from me.

Ps 19:8 The statutes of the Lord are right, rejoicing the heart: the commandment of the Lord is pure, enlightening the eyes.

Ps 50:16 But unto the wicked God saith, What hast thou to do to declare my statutes, or that thou shouldest take my covenant in thy mouth?

Ps 105:45 That they might observe his statutes, and keep his laws. Praise ye the Lord.

Ps 119:5 O that my ways were directed to keep thy statutes!

Ps 119:8 I will keep thy statutes: O forsake me not utterly.

Ps 119:12 Blessed art thou, O Lord: teach me thy statutes.

Ps 119:16 I will delight myself in thy statutes: I will not forget thy word.

Ps 119:23 Princes also did sit and speak against me: but thy servant did meditate in thy statutes.

Ps 119:26 I have declared my ways, and thou heardest me: teach me thy statutes.

Ps 119:33 Teach me, O Lord, the way of thy statutes; and I shall keep it unto the end.

Ps 119:48 My hands also will I lift up unto thy commandments, which I have loved; and I will meditate in thy statutes.

Ps 119:54 Thy statutes have been my songs in the house of my pilgrimage.

Ps 119:64 The earth, O Lord, is full of thy mercy: teach me thy statutes.

Ps 119:68 Thou art good, and doest good; teach me thy statutes.

Ps 119:71 It is good for me that I have been afflicted; that I might learn thy statutes.

Ps 119:80 Let my heart be sound in thy statutes; that I be not ashamed.

Ps 119:83 For I am become like a bottle in the smoke; yet do I not forget thy statutes.

Ps 119:112 I have inclined mine heart to perform thy statutes always, even unto the end.

Ps 119:117 Hold thou me up, and I shall be safe: and I will have respect unto thy statutes continually.

Ps 119:118 Thou hast trodden down all them that err from thy statutes: for their deceit is falsehood.

Ps 119:124 Deal with thy servant according unto thy mercy, and teach me thy statutes.

Ps 119:135 Make thy face to shine upon thy servant; and teach me thy statutes.

Ps 119:145 I cried with my whole heart; hear me, O Lord: I will keep thy statutes.

Ps 119:155 Salvation is far from the wicked: for they seek not thy statutes.

Ps 119:171 My lips shall utter praise, when thou hast taught me thy statutes.

Ps 147:19 He sheweth his word unto Jacob, his statutes and his judgments unto Israel. (his word: Heb. his words.)

Jer 10:3 For the customs of the people are vain: for one cutteth a tree out of the forest, the work of the hands of the workman, with the axe.

Jer 44:10 They are not humbled even unto this day, neither have they feared, nor walked in my law, nor in my statutes, that I set before you and before your fathers.

Jer 44:23 Because ye have burned incense, and because ye have sinned against the Lord, and have not obeyed the voice of the Lord, nor walked in his law, nor in his statutes, nor in his testimonies; therefore this evil is happened unto you, as at this day.

Eze 5:6 And she hath changed my judgments into wickedness more than the nations, and my statutes more than the countries that are round about her: for they have refused my judgments and my statutes, they have not walked in them.

Eze 5:7 Therefore thus saith the Lord God; Because ye multiplied more than the nations that are round about you, and have not walked in my statutes, neither have kept my judgments, neither have done according to the judgments of the nations that are round about you;

Eze 11:12 And ye shall know that I am the Lord: for ye have not walked in my statutes, neither executed my judgments, but have done after the manners of the heathen that are round about you.

Eze 11:20 That they may walk in my statutes, and keep mine ordinances, and do them: and they shall be my people, and I will be their God.

Eze 18:9 Hath walked in my statutes, and hath kept my judgments, to deal truly; he is just, he shall surely live, saith the Lord God.

Eze 18:17 That hath taken off his hand from the poor, that hath not received usury nor increase, hath executed my judgments, hath walked in my statutes; he shall not die for the iniquity of his father, he shall surely live.

Eze 18:19 Yet say ye, Why? doth not the son bear the iniquity of the father? When the son hath done that which is lawful and right, and hath kept all my statutes, and hath done them, he shall surely live.

Eze 18:21 But if the wicked will turn from all his sins that he hath committed, and keep all my statutes, and do that which is lawful and right, he shall surely live, he shall not die.

Eze 20:11 And I gave them my statutes, and shewed them my judgments, which if a man do, he shall even live in them.

Eze 20:13 But the house of Israel rebelled against me in the wilderness: they walked not in my statutes, and they despised my judgments, which if a man do, he shall even live in them; and my sabbaths they greatly polluted: then I said, I would pour out my fury upon them in the wilderness, to consume them.

Eze 20:16 Because they despised my judgments, and walked not in my statutes, but polluted my sabbaths: for their heart went after their idols.

Eze 20:18 But I said unto their children in the wilderness, Walk ye not in the statutes of

I your fathers, neither observe their judgments, nor defile yourselves with their idols:

Eze 20:19 am the Lord your God; walk in my statutes, and keep my judgments, and do them;

Eze 20:21 Notwithstanding the children rebelled against me: they walked not in my statutes, neither kept my judgments to do them, which if a man do, he shall even live in them; they polluted my sabbaths: then I said, I would pour out my fury upon them, to accomplish my anger against them in the wilderness.

Eze 20:24 Because they had not executed my judgments, but had despised my statutes, and had polluted my sabbaths, and their eyes were after their fathers' idols.

Eze 20:25 Wherefore I gave them also statutes that were not good, and judgments whereby they should not live;

Eze 33:15 If the wicked restore the pledge, give again that he had robbed, walk in the statutes of life, without committing iniquity; he shall surely live, he shall not die.

Eze 36:27 And I will put my spirit within you, and cause you to walk in my statutes, and ye shall keep my judgments, and do them.

Eze 37:24 And David my servant shall be king over them; and they all shall have one shepherd: they shall also walk in my judgments, and observe my statutes, and do them.

Eze 44:24 And in controversy they shall stand in judgment; and they shall judge it according to my judgments: and they shall keep my laws and my statutes in all mine assemblies; and they shall hallow my sabbaths.

Mic 6:16 For the statutes of Omri are kept, and all the works of the house of Ahab, and ye walk in their counsels; that I should make thee a desolation, and the inhabitants thereof an hissing: therefore ye shall bear the reproach of my people.

Zec 1:6 But my words and my statutes, which I commanded my servants the prophets, did they not take hold of your fathers? and they returned and said, Like as the Lord of hosts thought to do unto us, according to our ways, and according to our doings, so hath he dealt with us.

Mal 4:4 Remember ye the law of Moses my servant, which I commanded unto him in Horeb for all Israel, with the statutes and judgments.

Ex 18:16 When they have a matter, they come unto me; and I judge between one and another, and I do make them know the statutes of God, and his laws.

Ex 18:20 And thou shalt teach them ordinances and laws, and shalt shew them the way wherein they must walk, and the work that they must do.

Ezr 7:25 And thou, Ezra, after the wisdom of thy God, that is in thine hand, set magistrates and judges, which may judge all the people that are beyond the river, all such as know the laws of thy God; and teach ye them that know them not.

Es 1:19 If it please the king, let there go a royal commandment from him, and let it be written among the laws of the Persians and the Medes, that it be not altered, That Vashti come no more before king Ahasuerus; and let the king give her royal estate unto another that is better than she.

Es 3:8 And Haman said unto king Ahasuerus, There is a certain people scattered abroad and dispersed among the people in all the provinces of thy kingdom; and their laws are diverse from all people; neither keep they the king's laws: therefore it is not for the king's profit to suffer them.

Isa 24:5 The earth also is defiled under the inhabitants thereof; because they have transgressed the laws, changed the ordinance, broken the everlasting covenant.

Eze 43:11 And if they be ashamed of all that they have done, shew them the form of the house, and the fashion thereof, and the goings out thereof, and the comings in thereof, and all the forms thereof, and all the ordinances thereof, and all the forms thereof, and all the laws thereof: and write it in their sight, that they may keep the whole form thereof, and all the ordinances thereof, and do them.

Eze 44:5 And the Lord said unto me, Son of man, mark well, and behold with thine eyes, and hear with thine ears all that I say unto thee concerning all the ordinances of the house of the LORD, and all the laws thereof; and mark well the entering in of the house, with every going forth of the sanctuary.

Da 7:25 And he shall speak great words against the most High, and shall wear out the saints of the most High, and think to change times and laws: and they shall be given into his hand until a time and times and the dividing of time.

Da 9:10 Neither have we obeyed the voice of the Lord our God, to walk in his laws, which he set before us by his servants the prophets.

Heb 8:10 For this is the covenant that I will make with the house of Israel after those days, saith the Lord; I will put my laws into their mind, and write them in their hearts: and I will be to them a God, and they shall be to me a people:

Heb 10:16 This is the covenant that I will make with them after those days, saith the Lord, I will put my laws into their hearts, and in their minds will I write them;

Somehow, the cross caused our understanding of these scriptures to be tossed under the bus. I also have to admit that our interpretation of many of the same scriptures is not Hebraic, but rather Greek. We need to understand both.

Why do all these scriptures exist if the Messiah did away with all of them as a result of grace? If we are not hearing and obeying His instruction, whose instructions are causing all the confusion? Furthermore, how many scriptures can you find that suggest we not consider too strongly all the ones I just posted because *grace* was going to mean something entirely different after the death and resurrection of Messiah?

Chapter Nine:
Words, Pictures, Letters and Numbers

Nehemiah 1:9

But if you turn to me, and keep my commandments, and do them; though there were of you cast out to the uttermost part of the heaven, yet will I gather them from there, and will bring them to the place that I have chosen to set my name there.

Proverbs 7:1

My son, keep my words, and lay up my commandments with you.

Numbers, Numbers, Numbers!

Just for fun!

ELEVEN

If ten is the number which marks the perfection of Divine order, then eleven is an addition to it, subversive of and undoing that order. If twelve is the number which marks the perfection of Divine government, then eleven falls short of it. So that whether we regard it as being 10 + 1, or 12 - 1, it is the number which marks disorder, disorganization, imperfection, and disintegration. (Recommended reading: E.W. Bullinger's considerations concerning the number 11 found at philologos.org[1])

There is not much concerning eleven in the Word of God, but what is there is significant, especially as a factor. E.W. Bullinger was a dispensationalist; I do not agree with this idea. However, his study concerning the stars and numbers is extraordinary.

WORLD TRADE CENTER ATTACK SEPTEMBER 11, 2001 AND THE NUMBER 11

1. The historical event occurred exactly 7 days before the Feast of Trumpets/Rosh Hashanah on September 18, 2001. The attack on America was on the 11th.

2. The World Trade Center's twin towers standing side by side resembled the number 11.

3. The twin towers each had 110 stories.

4. The first plane to hit the towers was Flight 11 by American Airlines or AA. A is the first letter in the alphabet, so we have again 11:11.

5. September 11th was the 254th day of the year; 2+5+4 adds up to 11.

6. After September 11th there are 111 days left in this year.

7. There were 92 passengers on American Airlines Flight 11; 9 + 2 = 11.

8. There were 65 passengers on American Airlines Flight 77; 6 + 5 = 11.

9. The number of Tower windows: 21,800; 2+1+8+0+0 = 11.

10. The third building #7 to fall had 47 stories; 4+7=11.

11. American Airlines number 1-800-245-0999 1+8+0+0+2+4+5+0 +9+9+9=47 = 11.

---

1   http://philologos.org/eb-nis/eleven.htm

12. Beginning with American Airlines Flight 11, the other three planes had a sequential order:
United Airlines Flight 93. 9 + 3 = 12.
United Airlines Flight 175. 1 + 7 + 5 = 13.
American Airlines Flight 77. 7 + 7 = 14.

13. President George W. Bush went to New York on September 14, 2001 and spoke to the world from atop a pile of rubble that once was the World Trade Center now known as Ground Zero. The retired firefighter, Bob was standing with him and wore a helmet with the number 164 or 1+6+4=11.

I included this information simply for you to ponder. The bulk of information above was sent to me by email one day. I wrote an article based on the content.

When I began to learn about the Hebrew Alphabet, I had no idea what was about to unfold. I have since become fascinated with how the God of creation introduced to all of us a system of communication that is, quite simply, mind bending. In my quest to keep all of this book very simple to read, I wondered how this was going to be accomplished when I arrived at this chapter. (I want to start out by admitting that I do not speak Hebrew.

Prior to the year 1855, neither did most of the world.) The Hebrew language was reborn in large part because of the work of Eliezer Ben Yehuda, a Jewish man who lived from 1855 to 1922. Consider reading about him.

I need to digress for a moment and let me explain why. I don't have a shred of bigotry in my entire being. I sit at this desk asking my Savior to share with me so I can write this book. As I work to complete this task, I sense the vile hatred that exists in the minds of so many against Israel and the Jewish people. I recognize that the very Savior I speak of was Jewish to the whole world. How He was received by the religious leaders of His day is irrelevant to me when recognizing His choice to be Jewish. How the Jewish people of today struggle with His deity also is of little consequence to me. In fact, how any one of us interprets the Holy Scriptures is of little importance to me.

What is critical, in my opinion, are several facts that simply cannot be ignored or removed from our current reality. Israel was reborn into her ancestral home. The language of this nation was reborn. This people, including those scattered all over the world, never faded into obscurity. Every nation and every page of human history tells the story of the sons of Jacob in one form or another. If I am referring to Eliezer Ben Yehuda[2] or Theodor Binyamin Ze'ev Herzl,[3] or if I am revisiting the history of the Jewishness of my Savior on any level, it is because of who he is, not what we made him into. The Jewish people testify to what the God of Abraham, Isaac and Jacob set out to accomplish.

Similarly, men like Frederick Douglass, Jr. and Booker T. Washington, and George Washington all played a role in shaping our world today. The Judeo-Christian relationship was purposed in spite of race and ignorance. The United States became the most powerful nation on this earth, and Israel was reborn some 62 years ago. In these 62 years, the nation of Israel has become a giant in virtually every scientific field known to humanity.

---

2   Eliezer Ben Yehuda began to call for the restoration of the Hebrew language. Learn more by visiting: http://www.jewishvirtuallibrary.org/jsource/biography/ben_yehuda.html
3   Theodor Binyamin Ze'ev Herzl began to call for the restoration of Israel (Zionism) in the 1850's. Learn more by visiting: http://www.jewishvirtuallibrary.org/jsource/biography/Herzl.html

The slaves who came to this country were instrumental in what our Creator was accomplishing as well. I simply refuse to live in the rather shallow and all too oppressive fog of hatred and bigotry. My heart is sewn into every word in this book and if people would look past stupid, perhaps the glory of what is being done would come into view.

If you are a person of faith and think less of the Jews for any reason, this book is not for you. If you are black or any other race and you follow Christ, He is Jewish, so let's continue. When you know and understand the history of why God did what He did and with whom, it likely will change your personality and add to your humanity.

Now, let's continue. The Hebrew letters are the most amazing conveyance of biblical coding known to mankind, and why wouldn't they be? Just like the Messiah's calendar of events, times and seasons, as well as stars and galaxies, we have his alphabet. These 22 letters have a remarkable brilliance that reveals the nature of God himself. If you believe that God is unlimited, then please accept the fact that so, too, is all that his letters reveal. Before I go further I have to introduce the Paleo Hebrew Alphabet. But first, check this out!

בְּרֵאשִׁית בָּרָא אֱלֹהִים אֵת הַשָּׁמַיִם וְאֵת הָאָרֶץ׃ וְהָאָרֶץ |

the earth and   :earth the   and   the heavens   God   created   beginning the In

הָיְתָה תֹהוּ וָבֹהוּ וְחֹשֶׁךְ עַל־פְּנֵי תְהוֹם וְרוּחַ אֱלֹהִים

God   of Spirit the and   the deep   of face the on   darkness and   empty and   form   without was

מְרַחֶפֶת עַל־פְּנֵי הַמָּיִם׃ וַיֹּאמֶר אֱלֹהִים יְהִי אוֹר וַיְהִי

In the very beginning of the scripture, we see Yeshua (Jesus) on the cross in the meaning of the Hebrew letter *Aleph* meaning God and *Tav* meaning cross shown in the symbol surrounded by the box above, letter-symbols not translated into our English Bible.

Revelation 1:10
I am the Alpha and the Omega, the First and the Last.

135

John 1:11

In the beginning was the Word, and the Word was with God, and the Word was God.

When a person spends time learning the ancient Hebrew picture language, what is and always has been becomes astounding. The church did not teach any of this to us, largely because it does not know it. The following image is a chart of the Paleo Hebrew Alphabet.

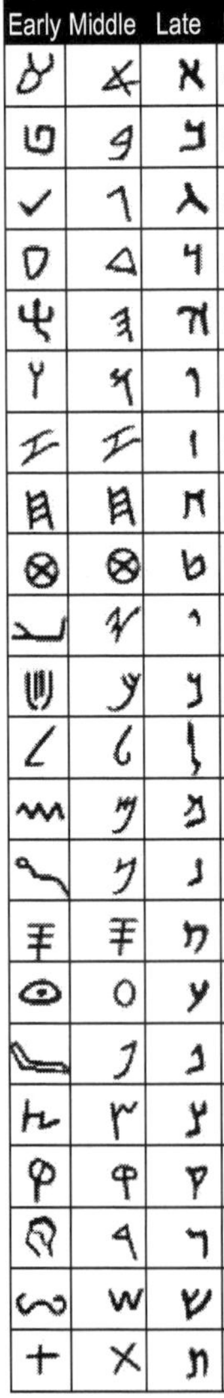
Early
Middle
Late

Ancient Hebrew				Modern Hebrew		
Name	Picture	Meaning Sound	Sound	Letter	Name	Soun
el	ox head	strong, power, leader	ah, eh	א	arrow	silent
bet	tent floorplan	family, house, in	b, bh(v)	ב	beyt	b,
gam	foot	gather, walk	g	ג	gimal	g
dal	door	move, hang, entrance	d	ד	dalet	d
hey	man w/ arms raised	look, reveal, breath	h, ah	ה	hey	h
waw	tent peg	add, secure, hook	w, o, u	ו	vav	v
zan	mattock	food, cut, nourish	z	ז	zayin	z
hhet	tent wall	outside, divide, half	hh	ח	chet	hh
tet	basket	surround, contain, mud	t	ט	tet	t
yad	arm & closed hand	work, throw, worship	y, ee	י	yud	y
kaph	open palm	bend, open, allow, tame	k, kh	כ	kaph	k, kh
lam	shepherd staff	teach, yoke, to, bind	l	ל	lamed	l
mem	water	chaos, mighty, blood	m	מ	mem	m
nun	seed	continue, heir, son	n	נ	nun	n
sin	thorn	grab, hate, protect	s	ס	samech	s
gah	eye	watch, know, shade	gh(ng)	ע	ayin	silent
pey	mouth	blow, scatter, edge	p, ph(f)	פ	pey	p,
tsad	man on his side	wait, chase, snare, hunt	ts	צ	tsade	ts
quph	sun on the horizon	condense, circle, time	q	ק	quph	q
resh	head of a man	first, top, beginning	r	ר	resh	r
shin	two front teeth	sharp, press, eat, two	sh	ש	shin	sh, s
taw	Crossed sticks	mark, sign, signal, monument	t	ת	tav	t

The ancient letters above represent symbols Moses would have used when writing something. The same is true for King David, with some slight variations. What has been translated into scriptures we read in the English (Western) church came from these letters, but the full meaning from the Hebrew may not have been conveyed. I believe the apostle Paul wrote his epistles in the Hebrew language as well, although by his time, it had evolved from what you see above.

When a word is transliterated, it basically is an attempt to find the closest match to a word in another language. The Greek translation of the Bible is full of transliterations, but the jots and tittles of the ancient Hebrew alphabet have not been translated into Greek.

Jots and tittles are variations in how a letter was drawn in the Hebrew language, whether it was made small, turned on its side, separated, or broken at one point. All jots and tittles have a purpose:

Matthew 5:18

For verily I say unto you, Till heaven and earth pass, one jot or one tittle shall in no wise pass from the law, till all be fulfilled.

There is so much being said in this verse of scripture, but if you are clueless as to what jots and tittles are and mean, you simply are reading a sentence that may not convey the accurate and/or deeper meaning of what was written in Hebrew.

Knowing the construct and deeper meanings found in the Hebrew Alphabet, which consists of 22 symbols, would make it possible to open up a literary world penned by God himself, with His finger no less.

When the first kings of Israel were ordained, they had to write a Torah scroll. They had to know God's system of writing and they had to teach what it said to the children of Israel. They would assemble everyone together and read the Torah scroll (the word of the Lord) aloud to the people. (I don't have the space or time to provide greater detail, but be encouraged to discover and learn more of this information for yourself.) The Bible is full of research material.

The following two articles are included in this book with permission from my friend, Dan Cathcart, whom I have known for thirty-five years. He and his wife, Brenda, are dear friends, and I strongly recommend purchasing two study manuals they have written to help fellow Christians take a second look at the glorious words of our Messiah. They are entitled *The Shadows of the Messiah in the Tanakh* (volumes one and two)[4] and are designed to incorporate the study of Torah and the Gospel into your own Bible study.

Both Dan and Brenda were instrumental in reshaping my approach on how to convey to fellow Christians a way to look back without offending them. I hope I am getting much better at doing this because, "You can't drag people to the Torah kicking and screaming." (Right, Dan?)

The Father pointed out to me that because of the transfiguration that occurred on the mountain with Yeshua, Moses, and Elijah, we followers of Yeshua are guided by the spirit of Elijah. I have realized we are to learn and share in his spirit, as opposed to trying to yank misunderstandings out of the chest of believers! Building bridges is far more in line with the Messiah's approach.

The Hebrew Letter "א" Aleph

This letter א is pronounced *aleph* and like all Hebrew letters, holds a meaning in itself. The sages say that the letters contain spiritual lessons and that the aleph holds a special place at the head of the Hebrew Alphabet. As the head, the aleph is said to be the "father" of the letters. As a matter of fact, the first two letters of the Hebrew alphabet form the word אב, pronounced *ab* or *av*, which is Hebrew for *father*. The aleph is also the first letter in many of the names of God found in the Jewish scripture, such as *Elohim* and *El Shaddai*, and as such, the letter aleph is said to represent God.

A cornerstone of Jewish theology is the *Shema* found in Deuteronomy chapter 6. It says in part, "Hear O Israel! The LORD our God, the LORD is One!" According to Rabbi Yitzchak Ginsburgh, the letter aleph, which represents God, is actually made up of three parts, or

---

4   *The Shadows of the Messiah in the Tanakh* - available for purchase through the El Shaddai Ministries web store: www.elshaddaiministries.us/storefront/sotmit.html

three of the other letters. It is made up of two yods (') separated by a slanted vav (ו). The yod means *hand* and the vav mean *nail* or to *secure*. So in the three components of the aleph, you see a hand above, reaching down, a hand below, reaching up and a nail connecting the two.

Another interesting fact about the Hebrew alphabet is that, unlike English, the letters also represent numbers. The aleph is 1, the beit is 2, the gimel is 3 and so on. When we look at the three letters that make up the aleph we find that they have a total numeric value of twenty-six (yod + vav + yod = 10+6+10=26). Then the logical question follows – does the number 26 hold any significance?

The single most common name for God in the Hebrew scriptures is יהוה. It is referred to by the Greek term *tetragrammaton*, which means *the four letters*. This name of God which first appears in Genesis chapter two has troubled Bible translators for centuries. The Jewish sages have no pronunciation of this name. When speaking it in public, or reading the scriptures, they will most often substitute the term *HaShem*, which in Hebrew means *The Name*. There is no official translation of this name, so in most English Bibles beginning with the KJV, it has been translated as *LORD* in all capital letters. You also may find it translated as *Yahweh* and *Jehovah*. The fact is, nobody really knows how it is pronounced because Hebrew has no vowels in its written form and no pronunciation marks are given where the יהוה is written.

Proverbs 25:2

It is the glory of God to conceal a matter and the glory of Kings to search it out.

So let's do a little searching and dig into a few interesting facts about these names of God and the letter aleph. As shown above, the aleph has a numeric value of 1 or 26 when broken down into its component parts. In the name LORD or יהוה we also have a numeric value of 26 (yod + hey + vav + hey = 10+5+6+5=26). So here in a single letter, the aleph, and in the most common name of God found in scripture, יהוה, we find the number 26 in both cases. But what about other names of God in the scriptures? Do they also add up to 26? No, but there is something much more interesting to be found in the text with regard to various names of

139

God. We are going to look at the first five verses of the Bible in the original Hebrew as we progress through this chapter.

A shortened form of יהוה used in the Hebrew text is י׳, pronounced *Yah* and the two most common other names are אל *El*, as in El Shaddai, and אלוהים *Elohim*. El has a numeric value of 31, Elohim is 86, and Yah is 15. Now, in the reference to Genesis 1:1 on the following pages, find the 15th letter, the 26th letter, the 31st letter and the 86th letter. Remember Hebrew is read right to left. What do you find? In all cases we arrive at the letter aleph! And as we learned from the sages, the aleph represents God, the head, or father. And you can add the Hebrew word for father, אב, to the list. אב has a numeric value of 3 and the third letter of the text in Genesis is an aleph.

In the original Hebrew text we find many such mysteries beyond our imagination. The LORD יהוה has given us such richness in His word, the perfect embodiment of Himself. Remember what is mentioned in the Gospel of John:

John 1:1 (MKJV)
In the beginning was the Word, and the Word was with God, and the Word was God.

NAM, Numeric Value

י׳ Yah, 10+5=15; the 15th letter of the Torah is א

יהוה LORD 10+5+6+5=26; the 26th letter of the Torah is א

אל El 1+30=31; the 31st letter of the Torah is א

אלוה א Elohim 1+30+5+10+40=86; the 86th letter of the Torah is א

אב av 1+2=3; the 3rd letter of the Torah is א

Genesis 1:1-5

בראשית ברא אלהים את השמים ואת הארץ והארץ
היתה תהו ובהו וחשך על פני תהום ורוח אלהים
מרחפת על פני המים ויאמר אלהים יהי אור ויהי
אור וירא אלהים את־האור כי־טוב ויבדל אלהים בין
האור ובין החשך ויקרא אלהים | לאור יום ולחשך
קרא לילה ויהי ערב ויהי בקר יום אחד

The Hebrew Letter "ב" Beit

The second letter in the Hebrew alphabet is the ב beit. Its meaning is *house*. In the ancient pictographic Hebrew it was a symbol resembling a tent on a landscape. (See the symbol on the following page.) It is interesting that if you turn this ancient beit 90 degreed clockwise it becomes our modern lowercase "b," the second letter in our modern alphabet.

In the original Hebrew manuscripts as well as Torah scrolls to this day, there are marks referred to as jots and tittles. Remember what Yeshua said about jots and tittles?

Matthew 5:18 KJV

For verily I say unto you, till heaven and earth pass, one jot or one tittle shall in no wise pass from the law, till all be fulfilled.

In the very first word of the Bible is what is known as a tittle. A tittle is an anomaly in the text, a letter that is larger or smaller than the others, a missing or added letter in a word or name differing from the standard spelling, a gap in the text, or even an upside down letter. Jots and tittles add a depth of meaning to the word of God that Bible translators over the centuries have chosen to ignore. In order to restore this deeper meaning, we have to go back and study the original text. So let's look at the very first verse of the Bible in the original Hebrew (Genesis 1:1).

Notice that the very first letter of the first word is enlarged. It is the beit, or the house. It is as if the entire body of scripture is flowing out of the house through the open door. Whose house is it? All the clues are in the very first word. The first word of Genesis in Hebrew is בראשית breshit (pronounced brasheet) and is translated into three English words: *in the beginning*. The first three letters tell us from whose house all these words come.

The second letter is the ר resh, and along with the first letter ב beit, they form the word בר bar, the Hebrew word for son. The third letter is the aleph, and we know that the aleph represents God the father. So from the house comes the Son of God. This is further established by looking at the other five letters of the word breshit. This is another Hebrew word,

141

תראשי resheth, which means *first fruits* and we know that the Son of God is the first fruits of the resurrection.

1 Corinthians 15:20 (NKJV)

But now Christ is risen from the dead, and has become the firstfruits of those who have fallen asleep.

In addition, the first three letters form the Hebrew ברא bara, which means *created*. Notice that this is the same as the second complete word in the Hebrew text. So God the Father, represented by the aleph א, with the Son בר bar, together created ברא (bara) the entire universe.

So we read the strange plural translation:

Genesis 1:26 (NKJV)

Then God said, "Let Us make man in Our image, according to Our likeness"

We now begin to understand the *Us* referred to here is God the Father and the Son together. This is not inconsistent with Hebrew thought.

In the Shema, a cornerstone of Jewish theology, found in Deuteronomy chapter 6 beginning with verse 4, and a part of the daily prayer life of a devout Jew, we find the Hebrew word *echad*, which is translated in English as *one*. But the word echad is in a semi-plural form. It represents a composite unity – a sum that is greater than its parts but is nothing without all its parts. The Father and the Son together are a composite unity who created (bara) the entire universe!

This concept of the Son being a composite unity with the Father is further illustrated in the Gospel of John.

John 1:1-3 (NKJV)

In the beginning was the Word, and the Word was with God, and the Word was God. He was in the beginning with God. All things came into being through Him, and without Him not even one thing came into being that has come into being.

The richness of God's word comes alive when we look a little deeper and come to understand it in its original language. When He comes to take us home, let Him find us in His house studying His words.

142

The Hebrew symbol *beit*.

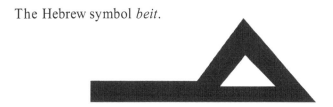

הָאָרֶץ	וְאֵת	הַשָּׁמַיִם	אֵת	אֱלֹהִים	בָּרָא	בְּרֵאשִׁית
The earth	and	the heavens	?	God	created	in the beginning

The information above can be found on the website Moed Torah.[5]

My entire purpose here is to show to you things that we were not taught in church. We were taught about the birth, death, and resurrection of our Savior. Did you know that these events all happened on His Festival days?

Leviticus 23 (New King James)
Feasts of the LORD
[1]And the Lord spoke to Moses, saying, [2]"Speak to the children of Israel, and say to them: 'The feasts of the Lord, which you shall proclaim *to be* holy convocations, these *are* My feasts.

The Sabbath
[3] Six days shall work be done, but the seventh day *is* a Sabbath of solemn rest, a holy convocation. You shall do no work *on it*; it *is* the Sabbath of the Lord in all your dwellings.

The Passover and Unleavened Bread (Death and Burial)
[4]These *are* the feasts of the Lord, holy convocations which you shall proclaim at their appointed times. [5]On the fourteenth *day* of the first month at twilight *is* the Lord 's Passover. [6]And on the fifteenth day of the same month *is* the Feast of Unleavened Bread to the Lord; seven days you must eat unleavened bread. [7] On the first day you shall have a holy convocation; you shall do no customary work on it. [8] But you shall offer an offering made by fire to the Lord for seven days. The seventh day *shall be* a holy convocation; you shall do no customary work *on it.*'"

---

5   Moed Torah website: http://moedtorah.blogspot.com/2010/08/hebrew-letter-aleph.html

143

The Feast of Firstfruits (Resurrection)

[9] And the Lord spoke to Moses, saying, [10] "Speak to the children of Israel, and say to them: 'When you come into the land which I give to you, and reap its harvest, then you shall bring a sheaf of the firstfruits of your harvest to the priest. [11] He shall wave the sheaf before the Lord, to be accepted on your behalf; on the day after the Sabbath the priest shall wave it. [12] And you shall offer on that day, when you wave the sheaf, a male lamb of the first year, without blemish, as a burnt offering to the Lord. [13] Its grain offering *shall be* two-tenths *of an ephah* of fine flour mixed with oil, an offering made by fire to the Lord, for a sweet aroma; and its drink offering *shall be* of wine, one-fourth of a hin. [14] You shall eat neither bread nor parched grain nor fresh grain until the same day that you have brought an offering to your God; *it shall be* a statute forever throughout your generations in all your dwellings.

The Feast of Weeks (Giving the Holy Spirit)

[15] And you shall count for yourselves from the day after the Sabbath, from the day that you brought the sheaf of the wave offering: seven Sabbaths shall be completed. [16] Count fifty days to the day after the seventh Sabbath; then you shall offer a new grain offering to the Lord. [17] You shall bring from your dwellings two wave *loaves* of two-tenths *of an ephah*. They shall be of fine flour; they shall be baked with leaven. *They are* the firstfruits to the Lord. [18] And you shall offer with the bread seven lambs of the first year, without blemish, one young bull, and two rams. They shall be *as* a burnt offering to the Lord, with their grain offering and their drink offerings, an offering made by fire for a sweet aroma to the Lord. [19] Then you shall sacrifice one kid of the goats as a sin offering, and two male lambs of the first year as a sacrifice of a peace offering. [20] The priest shall wave them with the bread of the firstfruits *as* a wave offering before the Lord, with the two lambs. They shall be holy to the Lord for the priest. [21] And you shall proclaim on the same day *that* it is a holy convocation to you. You shall do no customary work *on it. It shall be* a statute forever in all your dwellings throughout your generations. [22] When you reap the harvest of your land, you shall not wholly reap the corners of your field when you reap, nor shall you gather any gleaning from the harvest. You shall leave them for the poor and for the stranger: I *am* the Lord your God.'

The Feast of Trumpets

[23] Then the Lordspoke to Moses, saying, [24] "Speak to the children of Israel, saying: 'In the seventh month, on the first *day* of the month, you shall have a sabbath-*rest*, a memorial of blowing of trumpets, a holy convocation. [25] You

shall do no customary work *on it*; and you shall offer an offering made by fire to the Lord.'"

The Day of Atonement

26And the Lord spoke to Moses, saying: 27"Also the tenth *day* of this seventh month *shall be* the Day of Atonement. It shall be a holy convocation for you; you shall afflict your souls, and offer an offering made by fire to the Lord. 28And you shall do no work on that same day, for it *is* the Day of Atonement, to make atonement for you before the Lord your God. 29For any person who is not afflicted *in soul* on that same day shall be cut off from his people. 30And any person who does any work on that same day, that person I will destroy from among his people. 31You shall do no manner of work; *it shall be* a statute forever throughout your generations in all your dwellings. 32*It shall be* to you a sabbath of *solemn* rest, and you shall afflict your souls; on the ninth *day* of the month at evening, from evening to evening, you shall celebrate your sabbath."

The Feast of Tabernacles

33Then the Lord spoke to Moses, saying, 34"Speak to the children of Israel, saying: 'The fifteenth day of this seventh month *shall be* the Feast of Tabernacles *for* seven days to the Lord. 35On the first day *there shall be* a holy convocation. You shall do no customary work *on it*. 36*For* seven days you shall offer an offering made by fire to the Lord. On the eighth day you shall have a holy convocation, and you shall offer an offering made by fire to the Lord. It is a sacred assembly, *and* you shall do no customary work *on it*. 37These *are* the feasts of the Lord which you shall proclaim *to be* holy convocations, to offer an offering made by fire to the Lord, a burnt offering and a grain offering, a sacrifice and drink offerings, everything on its day— 38besides the Sabbaths of the Lord, besides your gifts, besides all your vows, and besides all your freewill offerings which you give to the Lord.

39Also on the fifteenth day of the seventh month, when you have gathered in the fruit of the land, you shall keep the feast of the Lord *for* seven days; on the first day *there shall be* a sabbath-*rest*, and on the eighth day a sabbath-rest. 40And you shall take for yourselves on the first day the fruit of beautiful trees, branches of palm trees, the boughs of leafy trees, and willows of the brook; and you shall rejoice before the Lord your God for seven days. 41You shall keep it as a feast to the Lord for seven days in the year. *It shall be* a statute forever in your generations. You shall celebrate it in the seventh month. [42]You shall dwell in booths for seven days. All who are native Israelites shall dwell in booths, [43]that your generations may know that I made the children of Israel dwell in booths when I brought them out of the land of Egypt: I *am* the Lord your God.'" [44]So Moses declared to the children of Israel the feasts of the Lord.

When you understand these Festivals you will begin to see that they are actually appointments, Yeshua's appointments whereby he will intersect with the Father's creation and do the spectacular. All of Israel is commanded to do them as a sort of dress rehearsal, a keeping of the record that was prophesied before it actually occurred. The Messiah said to the religious leaders, "You should have known" because they were practicing the very dates that he would come and Tabernacle with men.

A good friend, Eric Bissell of Oregon, is literally having revealed to him something that is so extraordinary I cannot even begin to write about it. Using the Paleo-Hebrew letters, he possibly is unsealing what Daniel was told to seal up.

Daniel 12:4

But you, O Daniel, shut up the words, and seal the book, even to the time of the end: many shall run to and fro, and knowledge shall be increased.

I encourage you to remember the name of Eric Bissell. You can go to the satellite/radio station to find more information.[6] Here you will find several guest appearances by Eric Bissell with Jamie Louie and Don Wyatt, who host the program speakers. In addition to Eric, many other teachers are presented to all of us as a result of the work that Don and Jamie do. I, too, have been a guest on the station. I hope you will check it out. I do not support every position presented on Torah 2 the Nations, but I categorically support what is being offered to a world where the Torah of our Messiah is being represented.

Messianic Judaism is another area on which to focus your attention, keeping in mind that all of us are lacking, but many of us are searching for our Hebraic roots to the scriptures.

---

6   Eric Bissell – visit the website: Torah2theNations.com.

Chapter Ten:
The Un-Colored Kids of the Kingdom

John 14:15

If ye love me, keep my commandments.

Un-Coloring Race is an attempt to share why your race is not an issue to the God of creation. The entire message is encouraging all of us to step out from behind the bigotry and perversions that are born as a result of the failure to obey the number one commandment: Love God and love one another. We are kids of a coming kingdom whom the Lord himself will teach.

Isaiah 54:13

All your children will be taught by the Lord, and your children will have unlimited peace.

These kids are to be seated before the Messiah as one people, un-colored and unbroken. They are those of us who stopped hating and hurting long enough to see the glory of our Messiah in every single breath

147

we take. This opportunity, though difficult, is what we call life. Whether we are passing or failing, all of us are participating, including those who came before us.

People quite possibly have been singing about brotherly love for as long as we have known about Cain killing Abel. None of us really know that song, its melody, or even the words. We all have been receivers of emotional and physical pain. Likewise, we all have inflicted emotional and physical pain onto others; we kill one another daily. I am hearing just now that twenty-three people died in an Iraq bombing. Twenty-three lives lost, twenty-three families ripped apart. Some days those numbers are higher, some lower. These stories blanket our news channels worldwide.

One planet, one people. I am reminded of a book and movie of the same name, *Lord of the Flies* written by Nobel Prize winning author William Golding. The book was published in 1954. The story calls to attention the miserable results of several youth, all boys, marooned on an island who attempt to govern themselves. Their noble aspirations deteriorate, leading to war and death in the camp. I was a little kid the first time I saw the movie. I read the book many years later.

In both instances, I remembered feeling sad for all of us. I was the child who, after watching movies of people suffering, would go into my room and cry. I think that being wired to love people (Thank you, Father) balances out some of the emotional deficits we grow up with. As I mentioned earlier in this book, going to George Junior Republic showed me that I was not alone.

All of us struggle in this world. Each and every one of us has obstacles to overcome. The most amazing thing about overcoming obstacles is the role other people play to help us to do it. Recently, my cousin's son was shot while sitting in his parked car. Only the person who killed him knows why. (He lived for a few days after the shooting.) Prior to this incident, he had lived for thirty-eight years, was soon to marry, and had asked the Son of God to enter his heart. Many people came to support and bring comfort to our family. In these days, none of us seem to be safely protected from others.

During the course of writing this book, I have met many, many people. My website, social networks, chat rooms, Facebook, and MySpace have opened up doors to connect with others electronically. My website[1] has links to many people who teach the scriptures, and I know most of them. The world seems smaller, and people closer. It is truly adventurous to be able to pop in and out of the lives of so many people via the Internet. Many of us want to have and be friends. Building a network of people is somewhat like going into a large grocery store and getting to know everyone else walking up and down the aisles. The idea that we now can push a button and talk to people dotted all over the planet while sitting in front of a computer really is fantastic!

Most of the people to whom I am speaking are people of faith. Most of us talk about our belief in the Gospel or the Torah, or both. (I believe in both as being one representation by the way.) Most believe in God, yet we all believe in Him differently. I suppose that those who believe in pornography or killing Jews are keeping us company on the internet, doing the same thing online in connecting with one another as do those of us who believe in the God of Abraham, Isaac, and Jacob. My point is that people are connecting to people in ways that were unheard of 30 years ago.

In my network, we talk about end times and prophecy, Christianity and Judaism. We talk about the right and wrong of a matter. (I have no idea what other folks talk about although I have had to work hard against looking at some of those other sites. It is amazing how easily abuse can occur in just about every area where flesh controls lives.)

It is amazing how diverse we all are. It used to be that one could only imagine what other people thought about any given subject. Now I can read snippets of the thoughts of hundreds of people daily. The world wide web offers a peek into the lives of people. Some of what we believe is comical, some surprising, and some terrifying. I never am bored at what people share, and the convictions they express while doing so. Nowadays people also fight with one another with a keyboard! At least that is better than guns or knives. Some days I feel like I am participating in the largest Jerry Springer audience ever! What I find truly most unfortunate is I feel like we all are part of the book *The Lord of the Flies*, at least at times.

---

1   Jeff Morton's website: www.hearandobey.us

149

I hope what I am writing here is causing many to take part in moving toward repentance. Like biblical Nineveh, we have an opportunity to change everything. A friend recently said to me, "Bad prophecy can be changed." When I listen to the words of hate coming from white supremacists or the so-called New Black Panther movement, or when I watch Muslims chant, "Death to Israel, death to America," I realize why we need salvation: we are a mess!

Women are being stoned to death and murdered because they are women. Twelve and thirteen year old girls are raped by their husbands, or others! People are being re-introduced to the worst form of slavery human history has known. You can't abort your child in some countries, but you can kill them for the sake of honor. What we do to one another is truly insane! The entire world needs to repent.

In the book of Deuteronomy, we find the Song of Moses.

Deuteronomy 32:

[1]Give ear, O heavens, and I will speak: And hear, O earth, the words of my mouth. [2]Let my teaching drop as the rain, My speech distill as the dew, As raindrops on the tender herb, And as showers on the grass. [3]For I proclaim the name of the Lord: Ascribe greatness to our God. [4]He is the Rock, His work is perfect; For all His ways are justice, A God of truth and without injustice; Righteous and upright is He.

[5]They have corrupted themselves; They are not His children, Because of their blemish: A perverse and crooked generation. [6]Do you thus deal with the LORD, O foolish and unwise people? Is He not your Father, who bought you? Has He not made you and established you? [7]Remember the days of old, Consider the years of many generations. Ask your father, and he will show you; Your elders, and they will tell you: [8]When the Most High divided their inheritance to the nations, When He separated the sons of Adam, He set the boundaries of the peoples According to the number of the children of Israel.

[9]For the Lord's portion is His people; Jacob is the place of His inheritance. [10]He found him in a desert land And in the wasteland, a howling wilderness; He encircled him, He instructed him, He kept him as the apple of His eye. [11]As an eagle stirs up its nest, Hovers over its young, Spreading out its

wings, taking them up, Carrying them on its wings, [12]So the Lord alone led him, And there was no foreign god with him. [13]He made him ride in the heights of the earth, That he might eat the produce of the fields; He made him draw honey from the rock, And oil from the flinty rock; [14]Curds from the cattle, and milk of the flock, With fat of lambs; And rams of the breed of Bashan, and goats, With the choicest wheat; And you drank wine, the blood of the grapes.

[15]But Jeshurun grew fat and kicked; You grew fat, you grew thick, You are obese! Then he forsook God who made him, And scornfully esteemed the Rock of his salvation. [16]They provoked Him to jealousy with foreign gods; With abominations they provoked Him to anger. [17]They sacrificed to demons, not to God, To gods they did not know, To new gods, new arrivals That your fathers did not fear. [18]Of the Rock who begot you, you are unmindful, And have forgotten the God who fathered you.

[19]And when the Lord saw it, He spurned them, Because of the provocation of His sons and His daughters. [20]And He said: 'I will hide My face from them, I will see what their end will be, For they are a perverse generation, Children in whom is no faith. [21]They have provoked Me to jealousy by what is not God; They have moved Me to anger by their foolish idols. But I will provoke them to jealousy by those who are not a nation; I will move them to anger by a foolish nation. [22]For a fire is kindled in My anger, And shall burn to the lowest hell; It shall consume the earth with her increase, And set on fire the foundations of the mountains. [23]I will heap disasters on them; I will spend My arrows on them.

[24]They shall be wasted with hunger, Devoured by pestilence and bitter destruction; I will also send against them the teeth of beasts, With the poison of serpents of the dust. [25]The sword shall destroy outside; There shall be terror within For the young man and virgin, The nursing child with the man of gray hairs.[26]I would have said, "I will dash them in pieces, I will make the memory of them to cease from among men, [27]Had I not feared the wrath of the enemy, Lest their adversaries should misunderstand, Lest they should say, "Our hand is high; And it is not the Lord who has done all this."'

[28]For they are a nation void of counsel, Nor is there any understanding in them. [29]Oh, that they were wise, that they understood this, That they would consider their latter end! [30]How could one chase a thousand, And two put

ten thousand to flight, Unless their Rock had sold them, And the Lord had surrendered them? [31]For their rock is not like our Rock, Even our enemies themselves being judges. [32]For their vine is of the vine of Sodom And of the fields of Gomorrah; Their grapes are grapes of gall, Their clusters are bitter. [33]Their wine is the poison of serpents, And the cruel venom of cobras.

[34]Is this not laid up in store with Me, Sealed up among My treasures? [35]Vengeance is Mine, and recompense; Their foot shall slip in due time; For the day of their calamity is at hand, And the things to come hasten upon them.' [36]For the Lord will judge His people And have compassion on His servants, When He sees that their power is gone, And there is no one remaining, bond or free. [37]He will say: 'Where are their gods, The rock in which they sought refuge?

[38]Who ate the fat of their sacrifices, And drank the wine of their drink offering? Let them rise and help you, And be your refuge. [39]Now see that I, even I, am He, And there is no God besides Me; I kill and I make alive; I wound and I heal; Nor is there any who can deliver from My hand. [40]For I raise My hand to heaven, And say, "As I live forever, [41]If I whet My glittering sword, And My hand takes hold on judgment, I will render vengeance to My enemies, And repay those who hate Me. [42]I will make My arrows drunk with blood, And My sword shall devour flesh, With the blood of the slain and the captives, From the heads of the leaders of the enemy."'

[43]Rejoice, O Gentiles, with His people;[a] For He will avenge the blood of His servants, And render vengeance to His adversaries; He will provide atonement for His land and His people."

[44]So Moses came with Joshua[b] the son of Nun and spoke all the words of this song in the hearing of the people. [45]Moses finished speaking all these words to all Israel, [46]and he said to them: "Set your hearts on all the words which I testify among you today, which you shall command your children to be careful to observe—all the words of this law. [47]For it is not a futile thing for you, because it is your life, and by this word you shall prolong your days in the land which you cross over the Jordan to possess." [48]Then the Lord spoke to Moses that very same day, saying: [49]"Go up this mountain of the Abarim, Mount Nebo, which is in the land of Moab, across from Jericho; view the land of Canaan, which I give to the children of Israel as a possession; [50]and die on the mountain which you ascend, and be gathered to your

people, just as Aaron your brother died on Mount Hor and was gathered to his people; [51]because you trespassed against Me among the children of Israel at the waters of Meribah Kadesh, in the Wilderness of Zin, because you did not hallow Me in the midst of the children of Israel. [52]Yet you shall see the land before you, though you shall not go there, into the land which I am giving to the children of Israel."

This is the record of Moses speaking to the kids born in the desert journey about the last generation of these people. Of the first generation of the Kids of the Kingdom, right before Moses is to die, he tells them about us. They proceed into a territory where killing and conquering is the order of the day. We are possibly (I believe emphatically that we are) living at a time when we need to be like these kingdom kids. However, and based on the atrocities that we meander through, half of us cling to rapture and the other half cling to dissention and division.

The Kids of the Kingdom of today do not have to go down in flames, if we choose to be like our first generation. Who are those kids today? Who are the people who can change the course of human history? Those people are any of us. We sit in front of a computer, networking our opinions and beliefs while life is (truly) in our blood. We have the power and the authority one by one to declare our allegiance to the coming Messiah. The adversary of humankind is trying to kill us all. We have been colored by our experiences, led away from being family to being separated by race, religion, and insanity! The enemy of the camp is sitting among us all, knee slapping and laughing all the way to the pit!

The world system is salivating at destroying Israel, just like the biblical patriarchs and prophets said would be the case. Those of us who have faith argue about the rapture, Judaism, Christianity and just about everything in between. Most of us are descendants of Abraham and yet we often act like the descendants of the fallen angels. The children that Moses was speaking of are facing annihilation; we are those children, and the Jews were to teach all of us the rest of the story.

Many wrongfully think this is an issue over the land of Israel. No, people, it is an issue over the children that became seventy nations; it is an issue to rob, kill and destroy. It is an issue whereby we forget our responsibility to love God and love our neighbor. We are those kids who are supposed to be doing what our faith encourages. The people of faith are no different than the people Sir William Golding wrote about in his book, *The Lord of the Flies*. This is a world-wide problem. *Un-Coloring Race* is about not being one of the individuals Golding wrote about.

Recently, I had an opportunity to hear Henry Gruver[2] speak again. Henry is a prayer walker. I first met Henry last year in Vancouver, WA. To be perfectly honest, I had never heard of prayer walking prior to that night. Mr. Gruver has literally walked all over the globe, praying. Last night Mr. Gruver spoke about his life, his testimonies, and that of his children -- two of his sons in particular. He shared a story about how one son tossed a rock, which severed the other son's eyeball. It was the sort of story that caused everyone in the room hearing it to grimace. I sat listening, all the while thinking "What causes anyone to walk all over the globe praying?" It would have been an easy thing to conclude that nutty people do stuff like that. Mr. Gruver has done this for nearly 50 years, starting at age 18; he now is 67 years old.

His son's eyeball grew back, the retina reattached, and to this day the eyeball of this child is perfect. This prayer walker prayed for a miracle many years earlier when his son was just ten years old and a miracle happened. The medical community, according to Henry, was astounded that something as impossible as an eyeball rebuilding itself could happen, and yet they watched this very thing occur over the course of five days. Mr. Gruver has story after story, testimony after testimony, concerning the miraculous as well as faith.

I stated in the first chapter I would have a surprise for you. The truth of the matter is I am quite surprised myself. During the course of writing this book, I have listened to many Bible teachers, Torah teachers, Rabbi's -- both Messianic and Orthodox, Christians, and non-religious Jews. I have listened to many speakers who love the God of the Bible.

I listened to Henry Gruver and came away realizing that God loves us all. Henry Gruver is a man who speaks as though you were sitting in his home, listening to a fireside chat. He is kind, gentle, and very unassuming in his presentation. At times, I was struck at how pleasant a man he is.

---

2   Henry Gruver's website: http://joyfulsoundministries.com

How does a person who has faced a myriad of trials and tribulation, death, and sickness prevail, and do so without the scars that so many people have inside?

I went to see Avi Lipkin[3] a while ago in Sumner, Washington. I have followed Avi's work for a couple of years. This man has criss-crossed the globe sharing a different message. His heart is not fearful of walking into any Christian denomination and sharing world events from his perspective. (There are others with different backgrounds doing this as well, and the God of the Bible is alive in every word they share.)

Avi Lipkin loves the God of Abraham, Isaac and Jacob. He does not cower when the name of Jesus Christ is mentioned. He does not sit in judgment for what the church believes. Avi Lipkin shares his life with the entire world. May many blessings be heaped upon you, Avi Lipkin.

Tony Robinson is my friend. I met him three years ago. Tony is a black man who teaches Torah. His website[4] is chock full of information that most in Christianity have never seen. Many in Judaism reject what he teaches. Tony shares how the Bible has themes and chiastic structures that reveal things found in God's word that stagger the mind. This brother is one of my favorite people in all of the Milky Way galaxy. (Who came up with that name, Milky Way?)

Tony shows the reader how to see parallelisms and themes that reveal Messiah, Jesus, Yeshua, Yehoshua Adonia...whatever name you prefer...in God's word. (Whether we call him Ben David or Ben Joseph or Christ matters not to me.) Tony Robinson shows you how to see him in virtually every page of scripture, and particularly the so called Old Testament. Tony Robinson is raising children. He and his wife sacrifice much in order for this servant of our King to do what he does. He is a child of the Kingdom and he is my friend. He could use your prayers, and do look at his work. You will be amazed at what you find.

I recently met Jeremy Gimpel, a young Jewish Rabbi. Jeremy recently visited our fellowship. Mr. Gimpel broadcasts a show in Israel called

---

3   Avi Lipkin's website: http://joyfulsoundministries.com
4   Tony Robinson's website: http://www.restorationoftorah.org

155

"Tuesday Night Live in Jerusalem." His website[5] shows that he is a man who loves the God of Israel. While Jeremy was speaking the other night I wanted to say, "Yes, we know!" You see, Jeremy was speaking about the Torah and the beauty found in it. It was obvious that he was not supportive of many of the pagan practices found in Christianity. (To be clear, neither am I.)

What was more obvious to those in attendance was his love for the God of Abraham, Hashem (which is true of most Jewish people, and with great respect). He showed in the scriptures how many would come to know the God of the Bible through the Jews. (Those who wrote the Bible were Hebrew, and virtually all were of the House of Israel.) Every Christian who follows Christ is following a Jew, so Mr. Gimpel is technically and spiritually correct. When I shook Jeremy Gimpel's hand, I shook the hand of a kingdom kid; I shook the hand of my brother. I also shook the hand of a priest by order of the scriptures. (If you think the Jewish people were replaced by Christians, I feel regrettably sorry for you.) Later, I was told that Jeremy Gimpel had been shouted out of a church while he was touring the United States. I won't mention the city or the church. I will say, however, that every person in attendance in that building is reading from a book that the Jewish people wrote. We must be bridge builders; otherwise, what makes us any different than the Muslim whose desire is to kill the *infidel*.

This man who is touring the United States of America is a bridge builder. Mr. Gimpel made the following statement: "We have been keeping the Holy Scriptures alive... for all of *you!*" This was a profound thing to say to a room full of Christ followers... A Jew telling us he loved us enough to keep the Holy Scriptures alive for us; it was a wonderful thing to say. The word of the Living God says the following in Jeremiah.

Jeremiah 16:19

The Lord is my strength and my fortress, my refuge in times of trouble. Nations come to you from the most distant parts of the world and say, "Our ancestors have inherited lies, worthless and unprofitable gods."

When one thinks of the lies that this verse is referencing, it becomes clear rather quickly it is the devastation religion has caused for millennia.

---

5   Jeremy Gimpel's website: http://www.thelandofisrael.com

Currently, Israel remains surrounded by nations that want to annihilate the entire country. The United States of America has literally fallen into a sort of debt that is impossible to repay and many in the country are divided socially, politically, and racially. At the same time, the world is calling on Israel to divide God's land. The entire world system is teetering on madness, in my opinion.

Black Americans overwhelmingly voted for our current president, as did many Jewish people. I am not a fan of the current administration. Moreover, I see the current administration as a sort of dress rehearsal of the revival of the Kingdom of Pharaoh, or even that of Jeroboam, the first king of the Northern Kingdom of Israel. While Israel currently is under a sort of unimaginable pressure to give up her sovereignty, the rulers of the world are lining up against her, just as scripture declares.

Islam is asserting itself once again, while millions of people across the world are being killed by war, famine, natural disaster, sickness, and/or disease. You name it and someone is living it, or dying as a result of what is happening throughout the earth. Muslim believers the world over are either dying for Jihad or praying for freedom. The majority are not marching in the streets to stop the killing. Mankind has spiraled into chaos on every level. We soon are to usher in the eleventh year of our newest century itching, it would seem, to blow the world up! Based upon the state of the world today, we are watching just about every abomination described in the Holy Scriptures becoming law, with many "Christians" participating in voting these laws into existence.

For convenience, children continue to be sacrificed daily. In today's world we call such sacrifices abortion. Islamic terrorism is criss-crossing the globe with the promise of 72 virgins as a reward for those who die. Islamic terrorism also promises to rid the world of Jews and Christians. The Unites States military is tired, while at the same time killing thousands of human beings who are committed to killing America. The world economies hang on to illusion and skepticism. War is not the answer, but it has been persistent for decades! (If I continue to list the madness here, my couch and my remote will lay siege on me, and I will spend the rest of the day miserable. This is what is happening to many of the Kids of the Kingdom as well.)

The Hebrew Roots movement and the Messianic groups popping up all over the world are "beating the hell" out of one another. Certainly not all are participating, nor do all fail to recognize what the Spirit of the living God is doing. Sadly, however, many are doing exactly what all religions do; they become religions. Nevertheless, as I learn about the Jewishness of Jesus and from the Jewish people what they believe and why, the truth... possibly the greatest weapon of all time, begins to disarm and destroy the lies that have separated us from one another. The Jewish people do not strap bombs onto themselves or their children in order to kill anyone. They may miss the mark like all the rest of us, but do you know any of these people? To date, I have found them to be some of the nicest people I have known in my lifetime. The lies that have been told about the Jewish people are truly demonic. Period!

As I leap at the chance to understand Torah, I also see how easy it is to go from one mess to another. As we go from one mess to the next, our nature is to govern by insanity. We need to stop, take a deep breath, and realize that all of hell is marshalling its forces against the God of Abraham. Those of us who admire King David and his slingshot are writing books such as this one, or touring the world trying to get millions to rally in support of the King's descendants. At the same time, those of us who admire Paul the Apostle are doing the same. We need to walk down this road together! These two men come from the same family. They both are distant relatives of Jacob. The sheer volume of what we see going on should tell us to stop and look. Amalek is chasing the rear and none of us are standing guard, or if we are, we are fighting about it!

Who are the *Un-Colored* Kids of the Kingdom? These are those who work tirelessly to uncover the lies we all inherited. The Holy One of God is calling you, calling all of us, to lay down our strife... and kick the enemy from the camp. I know that both ministries and individuals who line up behind the King of Kings and Lord of Lords and follow Him will be doing more for God's Kingdom than any other contributions we could make for ourselves and mankind.

The world is going to move against those who are building bridges. However, I am convinced that we are not to continue to argue over the right and the wrong of a matter but rather shake the hand of our brothers and sisters who are standing for the God of Abraham, Isaac, and Jacob and not let go.

The enemy of all that is occurring in these days is in the heart of the camp. He has been present in the garden, the tabernacle, the temple, the synagogue, and the church. The death of countless people continues unabated because we continue to let go of the hand of our brothers and sisters as we argue over doctrine and religion, race and politics.

This book could be about a lot of things I believe would blow a person's mind. I have witnessed people literally break down and cry over the revelation pouring out of the Bible. What I am learning as I study the entire book of the God of creation from a Christian perspective, Greek perspective, and finally a Hebraic perspective, continues to cause me to lose my breath! This wonderful book is about God's relationship, first to the Jews, and then everyone else. Whether you choose to believe this or not is a matter between you and God.

As I find original concepts in the ancient Hebrew language that I was not taught in Christianity, they are being illuminated in such a way that I have found a joy that nothing on this earth, so far, has been able to shatter. When I see and begin to understand God's plan and how He has dealt with mankind throughout history, I think, "What have we done?" When I look at the fighting that exists in all of God's families on the earth, there simply is no pain to compare it to. Likewise, when I think of what the Jews have missed, I realize the history of Israel is full of missteps. None of us are immune to being wrong when it comes to hearing and obeying a perfect God. I no longer want to point a finger at anyone who lifts up the word of God.

John 12:32
And I, if I be lifted up from the earth, will draw all men unto Me.

In the synagogue, the Torah scroll is lifted up, and it has drawn men to the God of creation for 3,500 years.

Adam knew Torah, Noah knew Torah, Abraham knew Torah, even Moses knew Torah before he received the commandments.

159

Exodus 18:16

When they have a matter, they come to me; and I judge between one and another, and I do make them know the statutes of God, and his laws.

The rebirth of Israel, the restoration of the ancient Hebrew language, and the Church world-wide wanting to know more about the Torah, is evidence of something far greater occurring than the coming tribulation. Make no mistake about it; we are entering a great time of distress. Nevertheless, our God is running the show. Those who are building bridges to him through the families on this earth will be part of the revelation. We must Un-Color ourselves from the hate and the division so we can see the nature of a very colorful God who colored his creation with beauty. We must return to the beginning so we will know the end with clarity. The end also is a beginning, for the millennial reign of the Messiah is at hand.

Christianity, from the perspective of the born-again believer, who truly has had a life-changing event with Messiah, is walking with the Spirit of the living God, and those who know Torah also have the words of the living God. The two groups are perhaps best represented by the bones mentioned in Ezekiel 36.

It is my belief that when Elijah takes his seat at the table, he will have millions of people who walk in the Spirit accompanying him. When the chair of Elijah is made ready, the words "This is the chair of Elijah" must be said in a loud voice (to quote Solomon Schechter and M. Grunwald).[6] Likewise, when Moses stands before the living God as happened in the transfiguration account, he too will possibly have millions of Hebrews with him. (Matthew 17:1-13, Mark 9:2-13 and Luke 9:28-36).

The House of Israel and the House of Judah are both being restored, and the two kingdoms are becoming one again, whether we understand it or not. The Kids of the Kingdom are becoming one also; one new man.

I am not of the mind that the two houses are tantamount to understanding who we are, as I stated earlier. It is *one* house, *one* people, *one* new man, *one* coming King. In the book of James, the author

---

6   Solomon Schecter and M. Grunwald wrote *Elijah's Chair*, © 2002 Jewishencyclopedia.com. For more information visit: http://www.jewishencyclopedia.com/view.jsp?artid=247&letter=E

addresses his letter to the twelve scattered tribes. He knew who they were, and they responded. This is why we know "The Rest of the Story" up to this point in time.

If you have not figured out yet, let me be totally clear, I am a person who absolutely, unequivocally believes in the deity of Yeshua the Messiah... even more so now that I am studying the Torah. As a black American, I realize that my color is not who I am, but rather a direct result of the choice made by my Heavenly Father. It was the idea of Him who created all of us; He make dirt live. As I watch the world spiral out of control, people literally destroying one another at a rate that is mesmerizing, I realize that the time Moses wrote about in Deuteronomy 32 is now. The last generation is a mess. To think of all of those who died faithful people, believers of the one God, the God of Israel, and realizing that I am purposed for such a time as this makes me feel privileged. I will spend the rest of my life sharing the wonder of it all.

If you are a Muslim who thinks that you can kill the Jewish people and take over the world, history is full of people who had similar thoughts. All of those who think this way are just that – history.

If you are a black American who loves Jesus but despises the Jews, it is an easier thing to shoot yourself in the foot as opposed to living a life against the God of Israel while sitting in the pews.

If you are a Christian who would say (and insist on doing so) that the Jews are blind, I would recommend that you stop carrying the book into your church which was written by the Jews. You have missed something for centuries.

If you are a Jew who does not accept the deity of the Messiah of 2,000 years ago, I don't blame you! However, you yourselves have had a miserable track record when it comes to obedience.

The best that we can do is to realize that all of us are actually a clump of dirt. Therefore, I suggest that all of us get together for coffee and talk about our kids! How much more can we learn about one another when we are simply being a part of one another?

The reality of our predicament is staring all of us in the face. One planet, one people, bent on self-destruction. We need a Savior to be sure. He has commanded us to love one another. We also need to repent.

From the depth of my spirit, I plead: Please join in with what the God of Abraham, Isaac, and Jacob has been leading all of us to do for centuries. Jews, Christians and all who would believe in the renewed covenant of Jeremiah 31:31-38, stop allowing the enemy to control the tempo. The madness of fallen man is rampaging against all of creation; it will get much, much worse if we continue to beat up on one another.

Whatever your beliefs, however you see the events unfolding in the country of Israel, her citizens are threatened with complete destruction. Nuclear weapons stand at the ready while the global empires of madness are under construction; they are combining into one (just as the very Jewish writers of the word of God so penned). The prophets of the living Tenakh did not make a mistake; Damascus will burn if we do not repent.

The *Un-Colored* Kids of the Kingdom are uncovering the lies that all of us inherited. The Ruach (Spirit) of God is flowing across the land and leading all of us back to Israel. His word declares it, and all of hell is going to try to stop us. The Kids of the Kingdom have had 6,000 years to grow up; our time to grow together has come! It is time for the children of Israel to march around Jericho again. We can electronically join with one another. What in the name of God are we waiting for? The answer is...Ben David, the Mochiach.

Jeremiah 31:31-38

[31]"Behold, the days are coming, says the Lord, when I will make a new covenant with the house of Israel and with the house of Judah— [32]not according to the covenant that I made with their fathers in the day that I took them by the hand to lead them out of the land of Egypt, My covenant which they broke, though I was a husband to them,[a] says the Lord. [33]But this is the covenant that I will make with the house of Israel after those days, says the Lord: I will put My law in their minds, and write it on their hearts; and I will be their God, and they shall be My people. [34]No more shall every man teach his neighbor, and every man his brother, saying, 'Know the Lord,' for they all shall know Me, from the least of them to the greatest of them, says the Lord. For I will forgive their iniquity, and their sin I will remember no

more." [35]Thus says the Lord, Who gives the sun for a light by day, The ordinances of the moon and the stars for a light by night, Who disturbs the sea, And its waves roar (The Lord of hosts is His name): [36]"If those ordinances depart From before Me, says the Lord, Then the seed of Israel shall also cease From being a nation before Me forever." [37]Thus says the Lord: "If heaven above can be measured, And the foundations of the earth searched out beneath, I will also cast off all the seed of Israel For all that they have done, says the Lord. [38]"Behold, the days are coming, says the Lord, that the city shall be built for the Lord from the Tower of Hananel to the Corner Gate. [39]The surveyor's line shall again extend straight forward over the hill Gareb; then it shall turn toward Goath. [40]And the whole valley of the dead bodies and of the ashes, and all the fields as far as the Brook Kidron, to the corner of the Horse Gate toward the east, shall be holy to the Lord. It shall not be plucked up or thrown down anymore forever."

Our hope, our destiny, our very reason for experiencing all of this is because the God of creation made a clump of dirt sit up and speak. He did so for his purposes. One day we will understand the gift that he brings on bended knee as a result. I always say "Thank you, Lord Yeshua, for making me to live as opposed to being a rock under the front porch!"

(Did you notice that in Jeremiah, He declares that the issue concerns Israel and Judah? He does the same in Ezekiel 36, 37, 38, 39... If I keep going I will end up naming every book in the Bible!)

If you truly are saved, and if you truly are born of the blood...you are a Kid of the Kingdom. That Kingdom is coming. It is coming to Israel, and we will be part of that Kingdom. Many in this world will not.

In fact, many are punished with famine and lack of rain for not coming to our kingdom in order to celebrate the Festival of Tabernacles. (The scriptures are speaking of the millennial reign of the Messiah.)

Zechariah 14:19

This shall be the punishment of Egypt, and the punishment of *all nations* that come not up to keep the feast of tabernacles.

The Jews, in my understanding of the scriptures, will be teaching us Torah along side of their brother, Yeshua, the King of the Jews.

163

Zechariah 8:23

Thus said the LORD of hosts; In those days it shall come to pass, that ten men shall take hold out of all languages of the nations, even shall take hold of the skirt of him that is a Jew, saying, We will go with you: for we have heard that God is with you.

Decide how deep your hate goes for the Kid's of the Kingdom. The price to pay is that you will be eternally separated from our royal family.

Chapter Eleven:
Black to B'reisheet

John 3:16

For God so loved the world, that He gave His only begotten Son, that whoever believes in Him should not perish, but have everlasting life.

The following information is provided by with permission.[1]

There are seven words in Genesis 1:1 in the original Hebrew (which is read from right to left). Seven is the number of spiritual completion. The act of creation took six days and on the seventh day God rested. (The Hebrew text below is read right to left).

את השמים ואת הארץ בראשית ברא אלוהים

In the beginning God created the heavens and the earth

The first word is pronounced in Hebrew *Breisheet*. It is from the word ראשית (re'shiyth) with an added ב (Hebrew letter bet) at the beginning of the word. This letter adds the meaning *in* or *through, because of, with*

---

1   Hebrew text, transliterations, and translations are provided with permission of moedtorah.com.

thought of. The rest of the word is רָאשִׁית (re'shiyth – Strong's #7225) means: the first, in place, time, order or rank, (specifically a firstfruit): beginning, chief(-est), first fruits, foremost. Thus, the word is translated *In the beginning.* But the word also can be translated two other ways. In the Hebrew thought, each of these translations adds depth of meaning to the word.

So we can translate Genesis 1:1 as *In the beginning, with thought of the Firstfruits, through the Foremost, God created the heavens and the earth.* This teaches us that God created the heavens and the earth with *Re'sheet* or with the purpose of Re'sheet.

Who is the Re'sheet or First Fruits of creation? He is Messiah as it says in 1 Corinthians.

1 Corinthians 15:20 (NKJV)
But now Christ is risen from the dead, and has become the firstfruits of those who have fallen asleep.

The first letter *bet*, בּ, in the original Hebrew pictographs was a house. Again, the first word can be seen as the *house of the Firstfruits.* So God's creation is the house of Messiah, His ultimate dwelling place, and through Him it was made.

Hebrews 1:1-2
God, who at various times and in various ways spoke in time past to the fathers by the prophets, has in these last days spoken to us by His Son, whom He has appointed heir of all things, through whom also He made the worlds; (NKJV)

He is heir of all created things, thus creation is the house of Firstfruits, which was created through him, the Foremost.

When Yeshua arose from the grave, the biblical Festival "Firstfruits" was fulfilled. He is the first to rise from the dead without a disciple or prophet commanding it to be so. We realize that Yeshua was in the beginning as well. Most of the messianic scriptures declare this to be true in all of Christianity. I agree. The only issue I have with the current culture of Christianity is that the original thought of the Hebrews is not taught. The example above should cause all of us to ponder the question:

"What else can be learned by returning to the ancient text in its original form," and certainly, "What is Paleo-Hebrew?"

Black to B'reisheet is about going back through the darkness that covered the deep, both in the beginning and when Noah released the raven, in order that we might reconstruct the light of the words of our of Creator through the Jewishness that revealed them. The dirt that produced all of us was not a multicultural creation, but rather the birth of a family. The bride is taken from the earth; we are that bride.

This book is not about the song, *We are the World* made famous by several musical artists including the late Michael Jackson; it is about learning our responsibility. We have been created for a purpose. It also is about realizing that the darkness manifested itself into all of our futures because of a poor choice and a lack of vision.

Proverbs 29:18
Where there is no vision, the people perish: but he that keeps the law, happy is he.

Mankind went from the Garden of Eden to an obstinate, willfully disobedient bride in a moment of sheer selfishness – perhaps with no vision. I think not, but we do the same thing today as did Adam and Eve. The eternal magnificence of the God of creation greets all of us with every continuing breath of life daily, and yet we choose death. The living dead cannot see, just as the dead cannot see!

Black to B'reisheet is not about black folk returning to the root of creation. This was not the sole purpose of my writing this book, although I hope many explore that concept. My underlying hope is that you, the reader, realize we all have dirt in common; all of us. We are made alive because of the *whom* as well as the *will* of our Creator. Surely Adam and Eve were given the ability to produce all the Kids of the Kingdom.

Far too many have left that identity as we rush toward the tribulation. I am hopeful that the tribulation does not come upon us before we realize our responsibility to return. Far too many are following world leaders instead of the world Creator. It is my prayer that the prodigal sons and daughters who comprise the bride of Christ realize our responsibility is to be prepared! We must return to the root of our purpose, to the root of the olive tree, to Yeshua, Jesus Christ. We must return to the story of Judah.

If you answered the previous question, "What do you know about the Jewishness of Jesus?" by responding, "Not much," this is the place to begin your trek. Black to B'reisheet is about coming out from behind the veil, and getting out of the darkness.

Jeremiah 44:28

Yet a small number that escape the sword shall return out of the land of Egypt into the land of Judah, and all the remnant of Judah that are gone into the land of Egypt to sojourn there, shall know whose words shall stand, mine, or theirs.

Get out of the nations! We are not of this world system; therefore, you must let go of the religions and the races that we defined. The Father (through the Son) produced the family of Jacob, produced an identity for them, and made known *the land* they were to claim, Israel.

Not one member of this family practiced Easter, Christmas, or Thanksgiving (and certainly not Halloween). To this very day and from the time of Moses, many of Jacob's descendants have practiced and celebrated the Passover, the Unleavened Bread, the Firstfruits, the Pentecost (or Festival of Weeks), the Festival of Trumpets, the Festival of Yom Kippur, and the Festival of Tabernacles...and so did the Lord Jesus! (You have to know why.) Again, Leviticus 23:1-2 clearly says that the Festivals are HIS Holy days, appointed times. He gives us this responsibility through Israel...always through Israel. He himself came to all of us through Israel, from the line of Jacob, to Judah, to David.

Black to B'reisheet also is about understanding the darkness of space, which declares the glory of the Lord. He declares in the following.

Genesis 1:14

And God said, 'Let there be lights in the firmament of the heaven to divide the day from the night; and let them be for signs, and for seasons, and for days, and years.

How many of you know this verse is talking about his desire to send to us signals to warn us? How many of you know why we have new moons or solar and lunar eclipses? The amazing phenomena of solar and lunar eclipses is not random. If you are computer savvy (or even if you are not), please find a way to watch the 50-minute presentation[2] in the footnote found below.

The information contained in this presentation has traveled around the globe (and continues to do so). It has caused quite a bit of discussion among biblical scholars, scientists, and folks just like you and me. The information unlocked as you reconnect to the Jewishness of the Lord will illuminate the construct of the Father's words in ways many of you have never seen... it will blow your mind! I pray that not only my fellow Christians will take the information in this book and investigate what I have shared, but all other readers as well, and that we all come to understand more about the bigger picture, especially in this hour.

Our responsibility is to hear and obey the Lord's commandments, for they lead us to safety. I have peppered this book with many of those commandments. These are written in His love letter to all His kids, all those born of His bride. (I have listed several in previous chapters.)

We truly are the remarkable kids of His coming kingdom. *Uncoloring* the races and the religions long enough to see who Jacob (Israel) really was is my heart's cry, and the purpose of this book. This man was purposed to produce a nation that would produce the birth of God himself in the person of Christ. The world system is attempting to divide His land again, just as it divided all of us from the purpose of our creation, and from one another.

Zechariah 14:

1Behold, the day of the Lord is coming, And your spoil will be *divided* in your midst. (The word *divided* has followed all of us through the centuries.)

2For I will gather all the nations to battle against Jerusalem; The city shall be taken, The houses rifled, And the women ravished. Half of the city shall go into captivity, But the remnant of the people shall not be cut off from the city.

---

2   50-minute video found on this website: http://elshaddaiministries.us/video/eclipsevideo.html

[3]Then the Lord will go forth And fight against those nations, As He fights in the day of battle. [4]And in that day His feet will stand on the Mount of Olives, Which faces Jerusalem on the east. And the Mount of Olives shall be split in two, From east to west, Making a very large valley; Half of the mountain shall move toward the north And half of it toward the south. [5]Then you shall flee through My mountain valley, For the mountain valley shall reach to Azal. Yes, you shall flee As you fled from the earthquake In the days of Uzziah king of Judah. Thus the Lord my God will come, And all the saints with You.[a] [6]It shall come to pass in that day That there will be no light; The lights will diminish. [7]It shall be one day Which is known to the Lord — Neither day nor night. But at evening time it shall happen That it will be light. [8]And in that day it shall be That living waters shall flow from Jerusalem, Half of them toward the eastern sea And half of them toward the western sea; In both summer and winter it shall occur. [9]And the Lord shall be King over all the earth. In that day it shall be—

This passage is talking about his kingdom, his people, his kids (you and me), and the Jewish people of the world.

Genesis 12:3

And I will bless them that bless you, and curse him that curses you: and in you shall all families of the earth be blessed.

Genesis 26:4

And I will make your seed to multiply as the stars of heaven, and will give to your seed all these countries; and in your seed shall all the nations of the earth be blessed.

What color are those nations?

Genesis 28:3

And God Almighty bless you, and make you fruitful, and multiply you, that you may be a multitude of people.

What color is this multitude?

Genesis 35:11

And God said to him, I am God Almighty: be fruitful and multiply; a nation and a company of nations shall be of you, and kings shall come of your loins.

What color is that company of Nations?

1 Chronicles 16:17

And has confirmed the same to Jacob for a law, and to Israel for an everlasting covenant.

So much for the Old Testament being made irrelevant as a result of the death of Christ and the birth of Christianity... unless, of course, the word *everlasting* is implying that the God of the nations of Israel (Jacob) is lying. I don't even consider that possibility, but far too many people have said to me that the Old Testament is irrelevant. In fact, you would be shocked at just how many people believe this. Read the following:

John 5: 45

For had you believed Moses, you would have believed Me; for he wrote of Me.

Luke 24:27

And beginning with Moses and all the Prophets, He explained to them what was said in all the Scriptures concerning Himself.

And, for the sake of driving my point home:

2 Timothy 3:16

All scripture is given by inspiration of God, and is profitable for doctrine, for reproof, for correction, for instruction in righteousness.

As you read this, realize that none of the New Testament scriptures were written when these statements were made. Think about this for a minute or two. In fact, think about it all day long if you need to. What we realize is that the Lord did not whip out a copy of the New Testament at any point during his time on the earth... He was restoring the first part of the book which led all of those people to him. The books of the New Testament are confirming what the first part of the book and the plan of redemption is all about. It is not a new revelation but rather the completion of a portion of the plan that began when God gave Adam and Eve the opportunity and the responsibility (through children) to recover from the veil that covered their nakedness after their disobedience! Their eyes were opened to darkness and blinded by darkness. Hence, the name of

171

this chapter, *Black to B'reisheet*, the beginning.

Identifying our Messiah four thousand years later is actually confirming the *firstfruit* and who he is, in living color! The story continues, and so do the appointed times, His Festivals.

When you return to the beginning with a mental shift` in how you process the Jewishness of Jesus, you will discover that the fourth word of the Bible is not translated because its meaning is not traditionally known. If you search a Bible dictionary, there is no definition associated with this word. Most Bible teachers are not aware this word even exists. (Remember, read from right to left)

הארץ	ואת	השמים	את	אלהים	ברא	בראשית
The earth	and	the heavens	?	God	created	in the beginning

This word is simply a two-letter sequence containing the first and last letters of the Hebrew alphabet, which are א Aleph (aw'-lef) and ה Tav (tawv). It is located next to the word *God*. You will not find this in Strong's reference.

Incidentally, the Menorah lines up under these 7 words perfectly. The center branch also lines up under the forth word and all other branches are connected to it. Learn about the Jewishness of Jesus. You will understand these very purposed features about how the word is written with profound clarity.

John, in the book of Revelation, is describing the center branch:

Revelation 1:12-13
Then I turned to see the voice that spoke with me. And having turned I saw seven golden lamp stands, and in the midst of the seven lamp stands One like the Son of Man, clothed with a garment down to the feet and girded about the chest with a golden band.

Yeshua (Jesus) calls Himself the alpha, omega, first, last, beginning, end, and this mysterious word underscores this idea by stating it in Hebrew. He is the Aleph and the Tav, the first and the last letters of the Hebrew alphabet.

My friend, Dan Cathcart, in a rather brilliant article "Hebrew Origins of the New Testament Scriptures" wrote the following:

I think everyone will agree that a language will reflect the cultures from which it emanates. The spoken and written language of a given people contains all the cultural idioms, syntactical structure, metaphorical references, and other content that is common to the people that speak or write it. A simple mechanical translation of one language to another renders largely gibberish. There are words and phraseology in one language that make no sense or have no equivalent in another because of these vast cultural differences. Let me give you an example: The Old Testament is largely written in Hebrew, and in the case of the Torah, the first 5 books of Moses, were written more than 3,500 years ago. When we translate the Hebrew into English, we go back to the Hebrew, read it and translate it word for word, right? Wrong! (Look at the figure). The Hebrew of Genesis 1:1 contains 7 words. When translated to English there are 10 words. Why is that the case? Now, look at the 4th Hebrew word; it is not translated at all! It is completely (and in all English translations) ignored. This is because this particular Hebrew word has no English word or phrase equivalence that can be inserted here and have any hope of creating a comprehensible English sentence. (See my post titled "The End is Declared from the Beginning – Part 4" for an explanation on my blog site at www.moedtorah.blogspot.com.)[3]

In translating these vastly different languages one to another, we have to attempt to ascertain the intent of the author or speaker and be able to relate that message to the intended audience. We have to know something about both the author and the audience, their culture, their history, their way of thinking, their value system etc. These all play into how a language is structured and how effective and accurate a translation will be.

---

3   Read Dan & Brenda Cathcart's work, as previously mentioned. Visit www.moedtorah.blogspot.com

When you begin to go back to the beginning, you will find that the Paleo-Hebrew letters open a window into how the Father laid all of his writings out in drawings. If you take my advice and learn about these letters, you will be changed! This ancient pictographic form of communication is what made all of this so easy to comprehend.

How many of you gave your children coloring books? They contain letters, words, numbers and pictures; so does the Lord's alphabet. He created kids and then he gave them books to read, sixty-six to be precise. He gave us the colors of the rainbow so we could do what all kids do, color our world, so to speak. What we did, however, was to do so in darkness.

Black to B'reisheet is about returning to the life that was purposed for the Kids of the Kingdom. Stop coloring his creation with racism, anti-Semitism and hatred. *Un-Color* yourself of these attributes; none belong to the King.

I strongly recommend the work of Frank Seekin,[4] and also that of Eric Bissell. I encourage you to go deeper into what they are sharing. Revelation is pouring out across the cosmos as we race toward the fulfillment of the very last book in the Bible. It is all relevant! This entire book is a peek into the very heart of Jesus. In his heart is love for all of us. He transmitted this in person to us as the Jewish High Priest of the Temple of Heaven. I am asking you to see His revelation from His point of view.

Jesus grew up in a Jewish household where the customs of what they believed reflected His commandments, statutes, and laws. His very character is inscribed in the descendants of Abraham. To say the way He reveals this is brilliant takes away the omnipotence of who He is. To see Him only from a Christian theological perspective is short-sighted. To learn about Him on virtually every page of the Old Testament is wisdom. A great deal of the Jewishness we don't know was purposed for us so we could know Him better. How ironic and diabolical that we simply are not taught on Sunday these revelations that serve to compliment the Gospels. As far as Sunday worship is concerned, halleluiah! He gave us seven days to worship Him, but I do encourage you to do so with the truth behind His Sabbath day and according to the Jewishness of who He is.

---

4   Dr. Frank T Seekins, author of *The Gospel in Ancient Hebrew*

The ancient children of Jacob's descendants did not keep the commandments, and yes they knew them, for Abraham knew them. Genesis 26:4-5 clearly tell us this. Moses' job was one of restoration, not initiation. They all returned to the root of the story. If we truly are the children spoken of in the Song of Moses, which the Lord gave to him, then we also need to return as the children of Israel with the Gospel of our Lord and Savior now revealed.

Deuteronomy 31:19
Now therefore write you this song for you, and teach it to the children of Israel. Put it in their mouths, that this song may be a witness for me against the children of Israel.

For the record, Moses obeyed.

Deuteronomy 31:22
Moses therefore wrote this song the same day, and taught it the children of Israel.

It is time for all of us to "Hear and Obey;" to hear and then to do is what leads to safety. The Lord did not discard these words; he lived them out perfectly. He performed the will of his Father with perfection as a witness to all of Israel. Your Bible is how they recorded it -- for *you*!

The Bible Cyclically Reveals It's Amazing, Living Word(s)

Each Paleo-Hebrew letter also is a picture, a word, and a number. The only thing to be added to these very peculiar letters is… us, the reader, as the bible has done in every century of its existence.

The lives of the people reading or recording these letters, pictures, words, and numbers are as integral as the entire message. This is the reason the word is living, and it lives through us. As a result of the "Life Gift," we are able to testify this moment that the breath of our creator is the air we breathe! This message is conveyed through those living the story. Their lives are the story, so we see a replay of the same story over, and over, and over again.

1) Joseph reveals himself to his brethren; Jesus (Yeshua) will do the same.

2) Haman's ten sons were hanged. Ten of twelve Nazi concentration camp generals were hanged also. http://www.law.umke.edu/faculty/projects/ftrials/nurembeg/meetthede fendants.html

3) Jonah goes to the depths of the earth and three days later is resurrected.

4) Noah passes over death into new life.

5) The Israelites pass over death into new life.

6) The baker and the butler with Joseph represented Bread and Wine.

7) The two men crucified with Messiah represented Life and Death.

Even the "Exodus" out of Egypt represents the trek of the egg through a woman. It moved through the Red Sea (fallopian tube), met the Life of the Messiah (Torah) (inseminated), and grew in the wilderness (womb) to become a nation (born).

The CHILDREN of the nation entered a NEW LIFE!

The earth is an egg attached to space. The Messiah is coming to impregnate the planet (the millennial reign) and for 1,000 years He will teach Torah (DNA). At the end of this time we will enter a heaven and a new earth. (Do you see a pattern here? How often has the birth of a child and the birth of a nation occurred?)

And so it goes.

The story is alive through the reader no matter what generation or century it is told!

Islam is raising up against the Nation of Israel just as did Assyria, Babylon, Rome, and (through Hitler) Germany. (The Church is part of the nation of Israel, but does not understand Torah, and the Jews are about to be restored to Messiah, but have YET to accept HIS Besorah.) The Lord is about to remove the veil during a great time of difficulty to come upon the earth. These things all have been raised up to judge the House of Jacob through Israel's disobedience to instruction.

The following article can be found at First Fruits of Zion's "Thoughts for the Week" located on their website (http://ffoz.org/)

The Birth Pains of Messiah

Vayishlach – חֹלִשִׁיו: "and He sent"

Torah : Genesis 32:4-36:43

Haftarah : Hosea 11:7-12:12

Gospel : Matthew 17-18

Thought for the week:

Rabbi Yochanon[5] (from the Babylonian Talmud) said "In the generation of the coming of the Son of David, disciples of the Sages will be few in number, and as for the others, they will see sorrow and grief. Many troubles and evil laws will be made, each new evil quickly coming before the other has ended."
(b. Sanhedrin 97a)
Commentary:
Rachel began to give birth and she suffered severe labor. (Genesis 15:16)

Jacob's beloved wife Rachel died while giving birth to her second son. The matter of Rachel's travail can be seen in a messianic perspective. In Jewish literature, the troubled times that precede the advent of the Messiah are called the birth pains of Messiah (Chevlei Shel Massiah, חבלי של) The birth pain imagery is from the prophets

---

4   A sage from the Sanhedrin folio: http://www.come-and-hear.com/sanhedrin/index.html#intro

Isaiah, Jeremiah, and Micah, who frequently used the "woman in labor" simile. The prophet Jeremiah calls it "the time of Jacob's distress":

Jeremiah 30:5-7

For thus says the Lord, "I heard a sound of terror, of dread, and there is no peace. Ask now, and see if a male can give birth. Why do I see every man with his hands on his loins, as a woman in childbirth? And why have all faces turned pale? Alas! For that day is great, there is none like it; it is the time of Jacob's distress, he will be saved from it."

In the Torah, "the time of Jacob's distress" that comes "as a woman in childbirth" is none other than the travail and death of his beloved wife Rachel. In that sense, Rachel's travail hints at the calamitous days of the birth pains of Messiah. Yeshua tells us the beginnings of those birth pangs will be characterized by wars, famines, and earthquakes.

In His first coming, the time of trouble actually descended upon Israel after Messiah's coming. The birth pangs the Master spoke of, including the destruction of the Temple and Jerusalem, came after His death and resurrection. The first coming was like a mother who births a baby, and after the baby is born, suffers through the pain of labor. This is in keeping with the words of the prophet Isaiah:

Isaiah 66:7

Before she travailed, she brought forth; before her pain came, she gave birth to a boy.

In Revelation 12, Israel is symbolized by a woman.

(Revelation 12:1)

"clothed with the sun, and the moon under her feet, and on her head a crown of twelve stars."

This woman alludes to Rachel. In the book of Revelation, she cries out, "being in labor and in pain to give birth." (Revelation 12:2) The child she births is the Messiah. He is taken from her up to heaven, and the dragon (satan) makes war upon her. In the same way, after Yeshua ascended to the Father, Rome made war on Judea and Jerusalem. The great travail came after the birth of the child.

Yeshua has ascended to the right hand of the Father. When He returns, His second coming will be anticipated by a time of great travail. However, the trouble of those dark days will forgotten in the joy of His appearing.

John 16:21

Whenever a woman is in labor she has pain, because her hour has come; but when she gives birth to the child, she no longer remembers the anguish because of the joy that a child has been born into the world.

(Thank you, First Fruits of Zion)

For the believer, it is time for the Coronation of our King and the marriage of the Bride. The Kingdom of our Lord is about to be born. Amen.

Be blessed this day.

Jeff Morton (http://hearandobey.us)

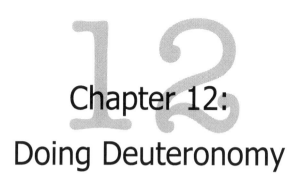

Chapter 12:
Doing Deuteronomy

Deuteronomy 30:11-16 (NKJV)

For this commandment which I command you today is not too mysterious for you, nor is it far off. It is not in heaven, that you should say, 'Who will ascend into heaven for us and bring it to us, that we may hear it and do it?' Nor is it beyond the sea, that you should say,

'Who will go over the sea for us and bring it to us, that we may hear it and do it?' But the word is very near you, in your mouth and in your heart, that you may do it.

See, I have set before you today life and good, death and evil, in that I command you today to love the Lord your God, to walk in His ways, and to keep His commandments, His statutes, and His judgments, that you may live and multiply; and the Lord your God will bless you in the land which you go to possess.

Who among you would live in a kingdom where nobody followed the rules? Well, probably most of us would not. From a king's perspective, who would want to be a king where no one obeyed the commands? I can't imagine too many kings who would welcome such a kingdom.

181

In a manner of speaking, or better yet, because of the reality of our world today, this is in essence what we all have. All of the nations are like the *Lord of the Flies* mentioned earlier. We are ruling and governing in chaos. We exist in a cesspool of curses.

I have completely pulled back from getting this book to the publisher as of this writing because of what I believe is being poured into this entire effort. Actually, the idea surrounding everything I have been doing over the last two years is beginning to reveal a certain continuity; a theme, if you will.

This book is an on-going revelation based upon what I am learning from my experiences. If I were to write down the levels of what I am learning as I return to the root of our Messiah, I would never finish this book nor accomplish anything else. There is so much about the Creator, who has purposed this entire experience, that losing my breath as often as I do is becoming much like breathing itself! I don't know how (nor do I want to learn how) to stop this from happening. I literally am having the time of my life. Nothing I have experienced thus far compares to what is turning up in my brain! This chapter is all about how easy putting all of this revelation into practice is – and practice we must.

Doing Deuteronomy is literally suggesting just that... *doing* it! The summation of all that was revealed to the nation of Israel is addressed in the book of Deuteronomy. The children born in the wilderness are about to go into a land purposed for them to inhabit. The rules of how the children of the nation of Israel are to conduct themselves are being reiterated by Moses.

Moses dies and Yeshua buries him. Think about that for just a moment...the Lord buries him and declares to all the following:

Deuteronomy 34:6
And he buried him in a valley in the land of Moab, over against Bethpeor: but no man knows of his sepulcher to this day.

None of you will ever find his body!

Jude 1:9
Yet Michael the archangel, when contending with the devil, he disputed

182

about the body of Moses, (and) dared not bring against him a railing accusation, but said, "The Lord rebuke you."

Are you all getting this? Think of the enormity of the blessing surrounding the name of Moses (Moshe). What does it take to have that sort of favor with Yahweh? *Doing Deuteronomy* tells us: "Keep My Commandments!" Look at this:

Deuteronomy 1:2
There are eleven days journey from Horeb by the way of Mount Seir to Kadesh-barnea.

Did any of you catch that? The desert trek from where they came out of Egypt and where they entered the land took eleven days to journey without a Cadillac (wink!). Why were they in the desert for 40 years? The answer is very, very simple. It took 40 years for them to relearn the commandments and then to do them! In fact, the children born in the desert were the ones who ultimately obeyed them (for a time anyway).

Joshua led the Kids of the Kingdom into the land flowing with milk and honey. I really am beginning to understand our responsibility. What is expected of us, the Kingdom Kids, appears to be very conditional.

Doing Deuteronomy is about changing how we think and how we do things. I would suggest to you that we have been coloring everything that we know from a cursed position. Our thinking is distorted; how we read the scriptures and interpret prophecy is all very, very skewed!

How often do we look at the colors of the rainbow with awe and amazement? Do we see the same thing when we look at the colors of our brothers and sisters? The reason we don't see the same brilliance is because of our skewed thoughts about one another. We are just as marvelous as is the rainbow, and more so, but we don't have the same reaction. This is what I mean when I suggest to you our view is skewed!

What is the second Commandment? Are you obeying it? I also suggest that all of the doctrines that follow so many of us through life have one common failure in that not one religion on earth is a blessing to the

183

nations of the earth, in these days in particular. All of us seem to be surviving curses.

I am sharing with you a snippet of what the Father is pouring into me about why I am writing any of this in the first place. A mental shift is occurring. I am asking you to consider what our responsibility is supposed to be. I am suggesting to you that it is very conditional. I am reminding all of us what the Kids of the Kingdom had to do in order to experience the presence of the King. I am pointing all of us back to the covenants. These are the requirements, the expectation, and we really do have to do them! I am offering a way to see the light through the darkness, but you have to choose to return. You have to understand *Black to B'reisheet* (going from a cursed perspective to a blessed perspective). Get out of the hole that has taught us how to live separated from the source of perfection. *Un-Color* your religion. It is killing us!

I was talking to a friend who happens to be a distant relative (descendant) of Booker T. Washington Junior. I explained how most of us know who he was. (If you don't know who he was then you have been robbed!) I thought to use the life of this brilliant man to demonstrate the blessings that follow his name through the pages of history.

The word of Yahweh says:

Deuteronomy 28:1-3

1"Now it shall come to pass, if you diligently obey the voice of the Lord your God, to observe carefully all His commandments which I command you today, that the Lord your God will set you high above all nations of the earth. 2And all these blessings shall come upon you and overtake you, because you obey the voice of the Lord your God: 3'Blessed shall you be in the city, and blessed shall you be in the country.'"

Booker T. Washington Junior's name has been lifted up. His accomplishments, his faith all are part of what we learn about when revisiting his life.

Most of us cannot name our grandfather of ten generations ago, but many of us know who Jacob's grandfather was. Of course, I am referring to Abraham. How is this possible? Again, the word of Yahweh tells us:

Genesis 26:4-5

[4]"And I will make your descendants multiply as the stars of heaven. I will give to your descendants all these lands, and in your seed all the nations of the earth shall be blessed; [5]because Abraham obeyed My voice and kept My charge, My commandments, My statutes, and My laws."

Most of the generations born through the centuries before us, beginning at the time of Abraham, know of this man. What a blessing! We know of his wife, the children, and the failures as well as the successes. We continue to learn the rules from Abraham. (Mr. Washington is remembered for his contributions, and respected because of how he conducted himself through extreme adversity. Hitler causes a far different reaction but he, too, is remembered.)

My point is that the Father says to the children of Israel via Moses (paraphrasing): Do this and I will do that. Don't do this and you will be cursed. The curses will chase after you! Look at our world today! We all are faced with consequences that border hell itself. Perhaps God's law (Instruction) was not done away with after all! I now know that it was not. What a diabolical way we have been deceived and thrown off course for two thousand years!

The curses are chasing almost every human being alive through life. Those who enjoy living in the curses will only enjoy doing so in this life. These folks will not partake in the kingdom, according to the words of Yahweh.

At the moment, actually for several days now, I have been stuck in the book of *D'Varim* (Deuteronomy). I am fascinated with the overall message. For those of you who were raised up in black families in America, the message is quite simple: You best behave! (You know what I am talking about.) Kids honoring their parents today is about as common as are harpsichords!

Isaac was in his thirties when he laid down upon the wood to be bound for sacrifice upon Mount Moriah. Two chapters later, he was getting married. (His reward, I suppose, for obedience.) Two thousand years later, perhaps Yeshua will be doing the same.

We have read about Isaac's life now for several centuries, a double portion perhaps. He was the father of Jacob, who produced the twelve tribes and the Lion of the tribe of Judah. In other words, look at what obedience offers. I simply am awestruck as to what the presence of the Father does in us and for us when we obey the rules. He is the all in all, including the blessings. This is what all who have obeyed his commandments have in common.

In the beginning of this chapter, I posted several scriptures from Deuteronomy 30:11-16. When I read this aloud during my studies, I heard myself utter, "This is too easy." In my spirit, I heard the Father say, "Yeah, I know!"

How many of us greet our day with these words: "Today, I am going to practice the rules of the Kingdom. I am going to get better and better at keeping the commandments. Today, I am going to understand the covenants that were established and the rules that govern them." The Father whispered to me "Very few of you do this. Just look at *your* kingdom; it is a mess!" For a couple of weeks now I have been asking men the same question, and all have said, "I don't do that first thing in the morning."

If you don't know what the Kingdom actually is, then you have been robbed! If you do know what the Kingdom is and don't follow the rules (based on Deuteronomy 28:15-68), ask yourself, "How many curses are chasing *me* through *my* life, and the lives of my family?"

I recently returned from Telephone, Texas (Thank you Craig and Murline Miles of Messiah's Truth) where I was invited to speak. While speaking, I realized how humbling it was to stand before people and share this message (or any message in God's word for that matter).

I have to share something that happened prior to my leaving for Texas in order that you may understand the full impact of why I am bringing this out. A few days before I was to leave, I was sitting at my computer and I most definitely heard the Father say to me in my spirit "Call your former wife; ask her to forgive you." I thought, "Why?" A few seconds later, in obedience I dialed her phone number; she answered. I explained to her that I was supposed to call her to ask for forgiveness for not keeping the commandments of God while we were married, and said, "Can you forgive me?" My former wife of 20+ years replied, "I am trying!" I almost went from zero to a billion degrees (which was common in our marriage) but the Father's voice whispered, "Nope, that is not why I told you to call her."

Anyway, while I was in Texas speaking (actually in front of people), it occurred to me the enormity and responsibility of speaking the words of the Father. I was truly humbled, really! All of a sudden during my presentation, I heard in my spirit, "Now do you know why I told you to ask your wife for forgiveness? The very feeling that you are having, the humbleness as you speak to this group of people, teenagers included, based upon your message, was not spoken to your wife or your kids."

I almost started to cry in front of these folks, because I understood. I understood that we men, we fathers, do not do very well and the curses follow our kids, our wives, our divorces, and our very lives. I got it! I understood why keeping His commandments is so critical to knowing Him and doing life.

Not doing so affects everyone and everything in our lives. You will walk out the consequences, if you are fortunate enough to be given that opportunity. My life, at the moment, is proof of this.

Something also worth noting about the day I called my former wife, Michele, occurred about two hours later. I went to deliver a CD to a friend. I was reluctant to do so because I had an issue about loaning out the CD, but I obeyed the Father's voice and took it over to my friend's house. As I was ready to leave, my friend handed to me six fifty dollar bills ($300.00). As soon as I took hold of the money, I heard in my spirit, "Thank you for calling your wife." Mind you, I do not promote prosperity doctrines, ever! I will say, though, that I knew this was a blessing from the Father. My friend said, "I have been procrastinating on obeying the Father."

Imagine, I was heading to Texas with no money. I ended up flying to Texas with money in my pocket, and the plane fare cost me less than $120.00 round trip from the Sea-Tac International airport in Washington State to the Dallas-Fort Worth Texas airport. I also was able to send a

187

gift to my daughter (who just turned eighteen), and pay a bill or two.

The things that are continuing to happen in my life are simply amazing! The Father always uses those who are willing to bless those who are in need. My list of folks to thank is becoming as numerous as the pages of this book. I really, truly am beginning to understand who we are in Him. I want His blessings for obedience to His commandments, and I look forward to more often being able to be one who is able to bless others.

Doing Deuteronomy is what we have to learn if we are to build a Kingdom with Yeshua. We have to practice in order to get good at it. We have to un-train *pain* and do a mental shift to obedience to His commandments, so we can stop presenting our lives as a curse before Yahweh, but rather as a blessing.

How do we do this? We all can start by learning the summary of the Father's commandments delivered to Moshe (Moses) and begin doing them before we dare to step foot into the Kingdom of Yeshua, the Messiah. We have to go back to B'reisheet in order to know all the rules of His Kingdom. We have to know Torah! Examine what you know; it does the body of Yeshua good!

In Conclusion

People of color are not a race of folks who survived slavery, or a people who have clawed their way back to some semblance of respectability. People of color are an idea of the glorious creator of all life everywhere. We have forgotten who He is, and certainly who we are in Him. We separated from the family, and in so doing, we created our own history, in a manner of speaking. Who we are is not defined by our neighborhoods nor by a police blotter. What we are is not defined by someone else disapproving of differing skin color. Those who do this practice sin openly, and with complete and utter disobedience to both the Gospel and the Torah found on every page of the Bible.

Likewise, the Jews (many of whom have left Torah) are not causing an entire segment of our population to want to wipe their families off the planet; sin once again is the culprit. Sin guarantees judgment.

(Have you ever wondered what radical Islam hopes to accomplish? Killing is how they have gone about it, according to history books, but then again, so did just about everyone else.)

Jews who want Israel, the land of inheritance, to be free of the Torah have an army getting ready to crash through the northern gate. It has happened many times before.

The God of Israel repeats his lessons over and over. In Hebraic thinking and writing, this attribute of the God of Abraham is meticulously demonstrated throughout biblical history. Many fellow Christians whom I have met with personally do not understand the Hebraic thinking of scripture. The revival we have talked about for centuries is quite literally occurring, but it challenges the status quo. The reason this is true, in my opinion, is because we do not know nor have we been taught to understand the patterns of Yeshua found in the word and the plan.

Just as the critical truths about our Messiah were revealed through his Festivals, the traditional holidays of the western world continue to

189

obscure why His Holidays matter. The people on both sides of the issue who refuse to rethink the cross guarantee another Haman and/or another Hitler. If God colored us purple (the color of royalty), and then we colored ourselves racially, can it not be said we kicked him to the curb and adopted the philosophies of the deceiver?

"Thou shalt not kill" is a perfect example of what we either don't remember or can't seem to hear and obey. What I have found over the course of these last four years is the significance of why He repeats His plan in virtually every generation. He shows us over and over what He is doing. He does this in a relational way with Israel. What He established with Jacob (and why He changed his name to Israel) is brilliant. If you don't know the Jewish concept of the inheritance of the firstborn son, then you cannot fully understand why the land many in Islam are trying to take away is the very land that was given to Judah by Joshua after they crossed the Red Sea. The city of Jerusalem is where the most prominent member of the descendants of Judah is to reign forever. (If this information is not in your memory, it is because you don't know the full story.)

The gods of this world are doing everything possible to stop the restoration of the inheritance from happening. Those who left Torah or tossed the Gospels under the bus, or those who live, eat, and breathe the New Testament alone, are clinging to a fixed point in time, not seeing a God of repetition communicating his identity in every generation through the plights of the nation of Israel. If the Jews would get this thing right, and the Christians would recognize the family we all are grafted into... we could get through this in a week! (Remember the six day war and the testimonies of those who fought it?)

People of color and people of religion are what we continue to be, for in today's world, we see everything revolve around the sun and think in terms of Science! We took ignorance and found a bazillion ways to prove just how right we can be about it. As a result, the gods/idols of this world take delight in our willingness to support their kingdom. They love the fact that we are not preparing to receive the Messiah's arrival. Some are preparing for a rapture, while others are simply preparing for the next election. Almost all of us are preparing for the next war. Bomb shelters and survival kits are flying out of production and off the store shelves.

We need to recognize the repetition coming around again. Just as Israel (the Northern kingdom) was taken into captivity by the Assyrian armies, and Judah (the Southern kingdom) was taken into captivity to Babylon, the consequences have followed the chosen people of God for centuries. King Saul, King David, King Solomon, and many others, fought off invaders who were sent by God to cause His chosen people to return to Him. It is happening again, although most do not recognize this cycle. Many don't know our Messiah was Jewish (for many reasons), while many Jews don't recognize this at all. So here comes another army from hell to bring us back to God's plan of redemption and salvation.

What is most ironic to me is that the latest generations birthed out of Abraham through Sarah and Hagar are sitting behind the news desks across the globe telling us that a war is coming to Israel, and the United States of America is burying its sons and daughters while trying to prevent it. The Judeo-Christian plan set into motion through Yeshua is fully under assault, and neither camp has yet to see the repetition of it all.

Meanwhile, the people of color separate themselves because of a false identity that was really the catalyst behind the Tower of Babel. We stopped following the God of creation, so he scattered the people, and the various races have perpetuated this repetition over and over again.

Every time I hear so-called Civil Rights pundits pop up out of the sin of racial bigotry and point the finger at one or more groups of people for the sin that is practiced in every race on earth, I realize how often we thumb our noses at the commandments of God. We jump again at the chance to take sides with those who have the best argument or the most fervent desire to survive such bigotry. Someone always dies.

Un-Coloring Race is a cry to Yeshua prior to the breach in the northern wall that is surely coming. It is for you to step back from what you thought you knew to re-examine the Bible from a perspective that reveals a very Jewish King. The King of the Jews is returning to a very Jewish land to restore a very Jewish family, and all those who have been grafted into the House of Jacob. Those who follow this plan will simply be going home. They will have a variety of skin colors, a variety of languages, and a variety of differences, yet all will be *Un-Colored* from the sin of mankind.

191

Learn about the root of your faith. He was born a Jew in Israel, and He coded into the first part of the Bible everything He wanted us to know about Him. He then showed up and proved it. He told us what He was going to do through the prophets Ezekiel and Jeremiah. He was rather specific, and He was absolute about with whom He was going to do it.

The *two sticks* represented in the book of Ezekiel (Chapter 37) tell of a scripture story that sets into motion Calvary (from a New Testament perspective). From a Hebraic perspective, the issue is about Judah and Israel coming together as one. A visual representation of the *two sticks* might drive the point home.   Ancient Hebrew — Taw / Tav / Tol

The Prophet is addressing the covenant promise made in Jeremiah 31:31-40. Understanding this focal point of the many stories found in the Bible about Jacob's descendants illuminates, and at the same time (hopefully) returns many of us to the original reason for the blood covenant so dramatically demonstrated on the cross.

Our Messiah was nailed to those "Two Sticks!" He died for a variety of reasons, and accomplished so much more than we usually are addressing, the sins of the world. He uncovered and uncolored the nature of sin by giving to the Nation of Israel his blood, which covers all of us in redemption. When you recognize both the House of Israel (Jacob) and the forgiveness offered to all of us through this family by one member, the Lion of the tribe of Judah, watch what happens to your mustard seed!

This entire effort is not about ignoring racism, anti-Semitism, bigotry, hatred, and injustice; rather it is about the root of all of these. That root is sin, and not race. See what Rabbi Paul (the Apostle) writes:

Acts 17:26
And has made of one blood all nations of men for to dwell on all the face of the earth, and has determined the times before appointed, and the bounds of their habitation.

The root to combat all of the above is Jesus, Yeshua, the Messiah. His root is the olive tree; we all are grafted in. Just as Yeshua was pierced in his side, so, too, is an olive tree when a branch is grafted[1] into the tree.

This book is not about looking at the societal failures or problems that are completely out of touch with the solutions found in the Torah and the Gospels. It is about being set apart, returning to the source who has asked of us to do just that, to be Holy. It is about knowing what that graft really, truly represents. My book to you is about *Un-Coloring* who we have become so that we might return to who we were meant to be.

View the following references:

Malachi 2:10
Have we not all one father? Has not one God created us? Why do we deal treacherously every man against his brother, by profaning the covenant of our fathers?

---

1 Wild olive trees possess something that cultivated varieties are lacking, unchanged and sustainable seeds. This attribute of wild olive trees makes them very desirable for local growers' orchards. To ensure that wild olive trees will grow in an appropriate climate, many growers will graft the branches of wild olive trees onto their established trees. This technique is known as topworking. Information found on http.//www.ehow.com/how_5766788_graft-wild-olive-trees.html

193

Luke 6:46

And why call you me, Lord, Lord, and do not the things which I say?

Isaiah 25:8

He will swallow up death in victory; and the Lord God will wipe away tears from off all faces; and the rebuke of his people shall he take away from off all the earth: for the Lord has spoken it.

The prophet Isaiah did not know what Christianity was when he wrote this and so... this book is about returning from the darkness to the light, from *Black to B'reisheet* or "In the Beginning." Christianity, Judaism, Hinduism, Buddhism, Islam, and everything else in between have failure within all of their respective beliefs because darkness is found in all of them. So much for man-made religion!

The King of creation is following His playbook for our restoration. Should we not, at the very least, collectively show a modicum of appreciation? The Koran was written in 600 AD (give or take a few years). The New Testament was written nearly 500 years earlier. The written law, Torah, was given to Moses approximately 1,500 years earlier still. The identity of YHVH was given to *dirt* and the *dirt* knew who He was.

If you agree that we should take a second look at why He came to this world Jewish, and why His parents were Jewish, learn about the Hebrew root and the study of it. Take a look at why He taught in the temple at the age of twelve (an honor only reserved for Jewish priests) according to what God (Yeshua) commanded Moses. (Read Leviticus; it all is right there.) Why did He pick twelve Jewish men to be disciples, and why did He send to them the Holy Spirit?

Return to the Hebraic mind of the Messiah, do a mental shift back to the beginning by embracing the Jewish people. To do so will undoubtedly cause a prophecy to be fulfilled, because the following will occur: "Thus said the Lord of hosts; 'In those days it shall come to pass, that ten men shall take hold out of all languages of the nations, even shall take hold of the skirt of him that is a Jew, saying, We will go with you: for we have heard that God is with you.'"

While my Pastor, Mark Biltz, and I were staffing our booth at the State Fair in Puyallup, Washington, he showed to a married couple the entire Gospel message found coded in the first word, *B'reisheet*. Their mouths dropped, and the husband put his hand onto his head and said, "My gosh, that is simply incredible!" Watching the Father open up the eyes of people, particularly Christians, is the most exhilarating experience of my adult life. I say this of fellow Christians because we know the Lord darkly. When this no longer applies, it blows your mind.

The Bible will give you the unlimited understanding of our King, if you are willing to take the book that Jewish writers recorded and see it from their perspective, not from the personal perspective of your box. He is out of that box and preparing to return to His people in Israel. They will cry out for Him, and so will you! Do you trust Him? He was a Jew!

When Adam opened his eyes, he did not see an Orthodox Jew or a Vatican Christian. When Moses saw him face-to-face, he did not see a Rabbi. When the Messiah came in the flesh, He came to the whole world as a Jewish teacher. This book is asking you to acknowledge this and then to go find out why.

THE LITERAL TEXT

by Jeff Morton

It occurred to me that none of us do what is asked of us, on a regular basis. I am beginning to think that all of this can be over in six days if we simply do them. Could it be that rest will occur automatically on the seventh? I use the war of 1967 as a gauge. I say *none* because we all are living the curses... see for yourself. The following words do not belong to me, or anyone of us, but they follow us through every generation. We keep choosing to experience the latter.

Deuteronomy 28

Blessings on Obedience

¹ "Now it shall come to pass, if you diligently obey the voice of the Lord

---

195

your God, to observe carefully all His commandments which I command you today, that the Lord your God will set you high above all nations of the earth. ²And all these blessings shall come upon you and overtake you, because you obey the voice of the Lord your God: ³"Blessed shall you be in the city, and blessed shall you be in the country. ⁴"Blessed shall be the fruit of your body, the produce of your ground and the increase of your herds, the increase of your cattle and the offspring of your flocks. ⁵"Blessed shall be your basket and your kneading bowl. ⁶"Blessed shall you be when you come in, and blessed shall you be when you go out. ⁷"The Lord will cause your enemies who rise against you to be defeated before your face; they shall come out against you one way and flee before you seven ways. ⁸"The Lord will command the blessing on you in your storehouses and in all to which you set your hand, and He will bless you in the land which the Lord your God is giving you. ⁹"The Lord will establish you as a holy people to Himself, just as He has sworn to you, if you keep the commandments of the Lord your God and walk in His ways. ¹⁰Then all peoples of the earth shall see that you are called by the name of the Lord, and they shall be afraid of you. ¹¹And the Lord will grant you plenty of goods, in the fruit of your body, in the increase of your livestock, and in the produce of your ground, in the land of which the Lord swore to your fathers to give you. ¹²The Lord will open to you His good treasure, the heavens, to give the rain to your land in its season, and to bless all the work of your hand. You shall lend to many nations, but you shall not borrow. ¹³And the Lord will make you the head and not the tail; you shall be above only, and not be beneath, if you heed the commandments of the Lord your God, which I command you today, and are careful to observe them. ¹⁴So you shall not turn aside from any of the words which I command you this day, to the right or the left, to go after other gods to serve them.

Curses on Disobedience

(Our current reality is based on living under this perspective. We continue to wallow in curses. Just take a serious look at the societies that we live in. *Un-Color* the freedom to obey the promise.)

¹⁵"But it shall come to pass, if you do not obey the voice of the Lord

your God, to observe carefully all His commandments and His statutes which I command you today, that all these curses will come upon you and overtake you: [16]"Cursed shall you be in the city, and cursed shall you be in the country. [17]"Cursed shall be your basket and your kneading bowl. [18]"Cursed shall be the fruit of your body and the produce of your land, the increase of your cattle and the offspring of your flocks. [19]"Cursed shall you be when you come in, and cursed shall you be when you go out. [20]"The Lord will send on you cursing, confusion, and rebuke in all that you set your hand to do, until you are destroyed and until you perish quickly, because of the wickedness of your doings in which you have forsaken Me. [21]The Lord will make the plague cling to you until He has consumed you from the land which you are going to possess. [22]The Lord will strike you with consumption, with fever, with inflammation, with severe burning fever, with the sword, with scorching, and with mildew; they shall pursue you until you perish. [23]And your heavens which are over your head shall be bronze, and the earth which is under you shall be iron. [24]The Lord will change the rain of your land to powder and dust; from the heaven it shall come down on you until you are destroyed. [25]"The Lord will cause you to be defeated before your enemies; you shall go out one way against them and flee seven ways before them; and you shall become troublesome to all the kingdoms of the earth. [26]Your carcasses shall be food for all the birds of the air and the beasts of the earth, and no one shall frighten them away. [27]The Lord will strike you with the boils of Egypt, with tumors, with the scab, and with the itch, from which you cannot be healed. [28]The Lord will strike you with madness and blindness and confusion of heart. [29]And you shall grope at noonday, as a blind man gropes in darkness; you shall not prosper in your ways; you shall be only oppressed and plundered continually, and no one shall save you. [30]"You shall betroth a wife, but another man shall lie with her; you shall build a house, but you shall not dwell in it; you shall plant a vineyard, but shall not gather its grapes. [31]Your ox shall be slaughtered before your eyes, but you shall not eat of it; your donkey shall be violently taken away from before you, and shall not be restored to you; your sheep shall be given to your enemies, and you shall have no one to rescue them. [32]Your sons and daughters shall be given to another

197

people, and your eyes shall look and fail with longing for them all day long; and there shall be no strength in your hand. [33]A nation whom you have not known shall eat the fruit of your land and the produce of your labor, and you shall be only oppressed and crushed continually. [34]So you shall be driven mad because of the sight which your eyes see. [35]The Lord will strike you in the knees and on the legs with severe boils which cannot be healed, and from the sole of your foot to the top of your head. [36]"The Lord will bring you and the king whom you set over you to a nation which neither you nor your fathers have known, and there you shall serve other gods—wood and stone. [37]And you shall become an astonishment, a proverb, and a byword among all nations where the Lord will drive you. [38]"You shall carry much seed out to the field but gather little in, for the locust shall consume it. [39]You shall plant vineyards and tend them, but you shall neither drink of the wine nor gather the grapes; for the worms shall eat them. [40]You shall have olive trees throughout all your territory, but you shall not anoint yourself with the oil; for your olives shall drop off. [41]You shall beget sons and daughters, but they shall not be yours; for they shall go into captivity. [42]Locusts shall consume all your trees and the produce of your land. [43]"The alien who is among you shall rise higher and higher above you, and you shall come down lower and lower. [44]He shall lend to you, but you shall not lend to him; he shall be the head, and you shall be the tail. [45]"Moreover all these curses shall come upon you and pursue and overtake you, until you are destroyed, because you did not obey the voice of the Lord your God, to keep His commandments and His statutes which He commanded you. [46]And they shall be upon you for a sign and a wonder, and on your descendants forever. [47]"Because you did not serve the Lord your God with joy and gladness of heart, for the abundance of everything, [48]therefore you shall serve your enemies, whom the Lord will send against you, in hunger, in thirst, in nakedness, and in need of everything; and He will put a yoke of iron on your neck until He has destroyed you. [49]The Lord will bring a nation against you from afar, from the end of the earth, as swift as the eagle flies, a nation whose language you will not understand, [50]a nation of fierce countenance, which does not respect the elderly nor show favor to the young. [51]And they shall eat the increase of your livestock and the produce of your land, until you are destroyed; they shall not leave you grain or new wine or oil, or the increase of your cattle or the offspring of your flocks, until they have destroyed you. [52]"They shall besiege you at all your gates until your high and fortified walls, in which you trust, come down throughout all your land; and they shall besiege you at all your gates throughout all your land which the Lord your God has given you. [53]You shall eat the fruit of your own body, the flesh of your sons and your daughters whom the Lord your God has given you, in the siege and desperate straits in which your enemy shall distress you. [54]The sensitive and very refined man among you will be hostile toward his brother, toward the wife of his bosom, and toward the rest of his children whom he leaves behind, [55]so that he will not give any of them the flesh of his children whom he will eat, because he has nothing left in the siege and desperate straits in which your enemy shall distress you at all your gates. [56]The tender and delicate woman among you, who would not venture to set the sole of her foot on the ground because of her delicateness and sensitivity, will refuse[a] to the husband of her bosom, and to her son and her daughter, [57]her placenta which comes out from between her feet and her children whom she bears; for she will eat them secretly for lack of everything in the siege and desperate straits in which your enemy shall distress you at all your gates. [58]"If you do not carefully observe all the words of this law that are written in this book, that you may fear this glorious and awesome name, The Lord Your God, [59]then the Lord will bring upon you and your descendants extraordinary plagues—great and prolonged plagues—and serious and prolonged sicknesses. [60]Moreover He will bring back on you all the diseases of Egypt, of which you were afraid, and they shall cling to you. [61]Also every sickness and every plague, which is not written in this Book of the Law, will the Lord bring upon you until you are destroyed. [62]You shall be left few in number, whereas you were as the stars of heaven in multitude, because you would not obey the voice of the Lord your God. [63]And it shall be, that just as the Lord rejoiced over you to do you good and multiply you, so the Lord will rejoice over you to destroy you and bring you to nothing; and you shall be plucked from off the land which you go to possess. [64]"Then the Lord will scatter you among all peoples, from one end of the earth to the other, and there you shall serve other gods, which neither you nor your fathers have known— wood and stone. [65]And among those nations you shall find no rest, nor shall the sole of your foot have a resting place; but there the Lord will give you a trembling heart, failing eyes, and anguish of soul. [66]Your life shall hang in doubt before you; you shall fear day and night, and have no assurance of life. [67]In the morning you shall say, 'Oh, that it were evening!' And at evening you shall say, 'Oh, that it were morning!' because of the fear which terrifies your heart, and because of the sight which your eyes see. [68]"And the Lord will take you back to Egypt in ships, by the way of which I said to you, 'You shall never see it again.' And there you shall be offered for sale to your enemies as male and female slaves, but no one will buy you."

WHAT DO YOU SUPPOSE WILL HAPPEN when we do what He asks? Yeshua offers to all of us the ability to do them... but, that same ability was given to Adam as well! And to Noah, Saul, David, Solomon, Moses, and Joshua. Adonai came and offered the same thing. We chose *Good & Evil* and died. Many of us have been doing the same thing ever since. He showed to us all what that looks like to Him and His father...while on the *cross* or the *Two Sticks* (Ezekiel 37:15).

Too many of us have not done what is required in order to teach the generations how to be blessed; *He* is that blessing!

Think about this carefully, really. Just think about it! As a result we keep repeating redemption instead of *living* with *Him*.

He entered into covenant after covenant, none of which were replaced, asking us to keep our end of the agreement through Israel. All of the covenants are made with this nation and her people.

Joshua 1:16-18

[16]So they answered Joshua, saying, "All that you command us we will do, and wherever you send us we will go. [17]Just as we heeded Moses in all things, so we will heed you. Only the Lord your God be with you, as He was with Moses. [18]Whoever rebels against your command and does not heed your words, in all that you command Him, shall be put

200

to death. Only be strong and of good courage."

Keep the commandments; hear and obey.

John 14:21

Whoever has my commands and obeys them, he is the one who loves me. He who loves me will be loved by my Father, and I too will love him and show myself to him.

John 14:23

Jesus replied, "If anyone loves me, he will obey my teaching. My Father will love him, and we will come to him and make our home with him."

John 15:10

If you obey my commands, you will remain in my love, just as I have obeyed my Father's commands and remain in his love.

1 John 2:3

We know that we have come to know Him if we obey his commands.

1 John 5:3

This is love for God: to obey His commands. And His commands are not burdensome,

2 John 1:6

And this is love: that we walk in obedience to His commands. As you have heard from the beginning, His command is that you walk in love.

What King would rule over a kingdom, via covenant agreements, for the benefit of his subjects, but the subjects dishonored all of them? What King would rule over his kingdom whereby none of the citizens of the kingdom obeyed his commandments? We have not kept any of the covenant agreements. We keep breaking the contract. He changed our hearts, and He will change the heart of Judah.

Un-color the lies that keep us cursing one another; it does the body of Jesus Christ our Savior, Yeshua the Messiah, good!

Thank you for taking part in my testimony! Now, Let's not walk in tribulation unprepared. Join with the Kids of the Kingdom and our Jewish brethren by supporting the land where His Throne will be established. His restoration of all things is nearing completion.

List of Hebrew Terms

The list of Hebrew terms and names are listed in order of appearance.

Torah —	The first Five books of the Bible written by Moses (Genesis, Exodus, Leviticus, Numbers, Deuteronomy).
Besorah —	Good News
YHVH —	Abbreviated name of God [Hand revealed, Name revealed]
Yeshua —	Original Hebrew name for Jesus or "salvation" in Hebrew.
Miryam —	Mary, the mother of Jesus.
Abba —	Father or daddy
Brit Hadasha —	The New Covenant
Elohim —	God
Adonai —	Lord
B'reisheet —	Genesis
Shema —	Hear and Obey (Deuteronomy 6)
Mitzvah —	Commandments or 613 statutes
Va'etchanan —	Hebrew for, and I pleaded
Eikev —	Follow or if you follow
Shlach —	To send or send out
Tanakh —	Acronym for Torah, Nevi'im, and Ketuvim
Nev'im —	The prophets
Ketuvim —	The writings
El Shaddai —	Might God
Hashem —	The name
Yahweh —	Transliteration of the name of God
Jehovah —	see Yahweh
El —	God
echad —	One
Moshe —	Moses
Ruach —	Spirit
Ruach Hokedesh —	Holy Spirit
Sanhedrin —	Ancient Jewish court (supreme court of Israel)
Ben David —	The warrior King to come (Mochiach)
The Mochiach —	The Messiah
D'Varim —	Deuteronomy

203

Resources and References

The following lists websites and footnote references organized by page number. Additional resources are included for further research and study.

ii Logo Design by Jimmie Christiansen: hamrinc@comcast.net
ii Website management by Ryan Anderson: www.ryancanderson.com
56 http://elshaddaiministries.us/audio/hayesod/20070827h9.html
56 http://elshaddaiministries.us/audio/hayesod/20070903h10.html
79 *Embracing Islam* by Victor Sharpe
83 The *Churchill White Paper* of 1922
84 *From Bablyon to Timbuktu* and *The Valley of the Dry Bones: The Conditions that Face Black People in America* by Rudolph Windsor
84 *Roots* by Alex Haley
85 *Myths and Legends* by Neil Philip
87 *Content of Character* idea by Dr. Martim Luther King, Jr.
92 *The Mysteries of Mithra* by Frank Cumont: http://www.near-death.com/experiences/origen048.html
92 *Truth of Tradition* DVD by Jim Staley: www.passionfortruth.com
110 Wikipedia. web reference to Shema: http://en.wikipedia.org/wiki/Shema_Yisrael
110 YoutTube video of Shema: http://www.youtube.com/watch?v=Fzvkr1RNZK8
111 *Creation's Heartbeat* by Dr. Yonathan Fass
112 *Enmity Between the Seed* by Bill Cloud
132 Considerations concerning the number 11 found at: http://philologos.org/eb-nis/eleven.htm
134 http://www.jewishvirtuallibrary.org/jsource/biography/ben_yehuda.html
134 http://www.jewishvirtuallibrary.org/jsource/biography/Herzl.html
138 *The Shadows of the Messiah in the Tanakh*: www.elshaddaiministries.us/storefront/sotmit.html
143 Moed Torah website: http://moedtorah.blogspot.com/2010/08/hebrew-letter-aleph.html
146 Eric Bissell website information: website: Torah2theNations.com
148 William Golding wrote *The Lord of the Flies*
149 Jeff Morton's website: www.hearandobey.com
154 Henry Gruver's website: http://joyfulsoundministries.com
155 Avi Lipkin's website: http://www.vicmord.com
155 Tony Robinson's website: http://www.restorationoftorah.org
156 Jeremy Gimpel's website: http://www.thelandofisrael.com
160 http://www.jewishencyclopedia.com/view.jsp?artid=247&letter=E
165 For further study in the Hebrew language, visit moedtorah.com
169 50-minute video from El Shaddai ministries
173 Cathcart's article "Hebrew Origins of the New Testament Scriptures" on www.moedtorah.com
174 Dr. Frank T Seekins, author of *The Gospel in Ancient Hebrew*
176 http://www.law.umke.edu/faculty/projects/ftrials/nurembeg/meetthedefendants.html
177 First Fruits of Zion's *Thoughts for the Week*: http://ffoz.org/
177 Rabbi Yochanon on http://www.come-and-hear.com/sanhedrin/index.html#intro
184 Booker T. Washington, Jr.
193 Grafting information: http.//www.ehow.com/how_5766788_graft-wild-olive-trees.html

Websites

- Bible Jolts, Dr. Yonathon Fass: http://Biblejolts.org/
- Shoreshim Ministries, Bill Cloud: http://www.billcloud.org
- Wildbranch Ministries, Brad Scott: http://www.wildbranch.org/
- First Fruits of Zion: http://ffoz.org/

- God's Learning Channel [Primetime Christian Broadcasting]: http://www.godslearningchannel.com/
- Love for Israel Conferences, Hank & Marilee Hobson: http://www.love-4-israel.com/
- Joyful sound Ministries, Henry Gruver: http://joyfulsoundministries.com
- Hearing and Obeying, Jeff Morton: http://www.hearandobey.us
- Passion for Truth Ministries, Jim Staley: http://www.passionfortruth.com/
- El Shaddai Ministries, Mark Biltz: http://www.elshaddaiministries.us
- Moed Torah, Dan & Brenda Cathcart: http://moedtorah.blogspot.com
- Near death experiences and the afterlife: http://www.near-death.com/index.html
- Wisdom in Torah, Rico Cortes: http://www.wisdomintorah.com
- Restoration of Torah Ministries, Tony Robinson: http://www.restorationoftorah.org
- Discovering Hebrew roots through Torah truth: http://www.wisdomintorah.com

Recommended informational DVD's

- *The Feasts of the Lord*, by Mark Biltz of El Shaddai Ministries
- *Studies in our Hebrew Roots* Volumes 1&2, By Mark Biltz of El Shaddai Ministries
- Bill Cloud (anything that you can get your hands on)
- Jim Staley: *Identity Crisis* and *Truth or Tradition*
- Louie Giglio's *"How Great Is Our God"* and *"Indescribable"*

Source Notes (Bibliography)

1. All stories in this publication are factual as recalled by the author.

2. James Strong, *Strong's Exhaustive Concordance of the Bible* (Nashville, TN: Thomas Nelson Publishers, ©1995, 1996)

3. Michael Peter (Stone) Engelbrite, *American King James Version* (AKJV) of the Holy Bible. (Published by Inspired Idea: the AKJV version of the Holy Bible placed in public domain November 8, 1999)

4. Scripture taken from the *New King James Version* (NKJV) of the Bible (Nashville, TN, Thomas Nelson, Inc. ©1982) Used by permission. All rights reserved.

5. Alex Haley, *Roots* (New York: Bantam Doubleday Dell Publishing Group, Inc, ©1974)

7. Neil Phillips, *Illustrated Book of Myths* (London, DK Publishing, ©1995)

8. Rudolph R Windsor, *From Babylon to Timbuktu* (Atlanta, GA: Windsor's Golden Series, 1st edition ©1969. 19th edition ©2003)

9. Rudolph R Windsor, *The Valley of Dry Bones* (Atlanta, GA: Windsor's Golden Series, ©1986, 1988)

10. Dr Yonathan Fass, *Creation's Heartbeat: The Bible's Entry Code in Genesis 1:1* (Laytonsville, MD: Ottorvf distributed by Gardner's, ©2009)

11. Murline Miles, *Let Yahshua Rock Your World* (Allen, TX: Messiah's Truth, ©2009)

12. Victor Sharpe, *Politicide*, volumes I and II (Raleigh, NC Lulu Press, ©2004)

13. Bill Cloud, *Enmity between the Seeds* (Cleveland, TN, Voice of Evangelism - Bayou Press, ©2004)

14. Catherine Clinton, *Harriet Tubman: The Road to Freedom* (New York: Little, Brown, and Company/Back Bay Books, ©2004, 2005)

15. Frederick Douglas Jr, "A Narrative of the Life of Frederick Douglass." The Anti Slavery Office, 1845

16. B. L. Abrahams, essay entitled, "The Expulsion of the Jews from England 1290" (Library of California)

17. Riley H Nelson, *Replacement Theology* (Longwood, FL: Xulon Press, ©2008)

18. Barry E. Horner, *Future Israel: Why Christian Anti-Judaism Must Be Challenged* (Nashville, TN: B&H Publishing Group, ©2007)

19. Frank M. Snowden, Jr., *Blacks in Antiquity: Ethiopians in the Greco-Roman Experience* (Cambridge, MA: Belknap Press of Harvard University Press, ©1970, 13th printing ©2000)

20. Frank M. Snowden, *Before Color Prejudice: The Ancient Views of Blacks* (Cambridge, MA: Harvard University Press, ©1983, 1991)

21. Phil Lindner, *Power Bible CD* (Bronson, MI: Online Publishing, Inc. ©2007) Used by permission. All rights reserved.

22. Victor Schlatter, *Nineveh: A Parody of the Present* (Mobil, AL: Evergreen Press, ©2009)

Un-Coloring Race
BLACK TO B'REISHEET
Testimony of a Black Christian American

JEFF S. MORTON

www.hearandobey.us
Gig Harbor, WA

Made in the USA
Columbia, SC
26 August 2021